JOURNEY TO MY SELF

Annie McCaffry has been an international lecturer and seminar leader for twenty years and has practices in London and in Wiltshire, where she now lives. She combines her learned skills, her humour, and her inituitive ability to diagnose the causes of disease, and works closely with doctors and psychologists.

Journey to My Self

THE HEALING OF RELATIONSHIPS
AND THE TRANSFORMATION
OF FAMILY PATTERNS

ANNIE McCAFFRY

ELEMENT
Shaftesbury, Dorset ● Rockport, Massachusetts
Brisbane, Queensland

© Annie McCaffry 1992

Published in Great Britain in 1992 by
Element Books Limited
Longmead, Shaftesbury, Dorset

Published in the USA in 1992 by
Element, Inc
42 Broadway, Rockport, MA 01966

Published in Australia in 1992 by
Element Books Limited for
Jacaranda Wiley Limited
33 Park Road, Milton, Brisbane 4064

Cover design by Barbara McGavin
Designed by Roger Lightfoot
Typeset by Colset Private Limited, Singapore
Printed and bound in Great Britain by
Dotesios Ltd, Trowbridge, Wiltshire

British Library Cataloguing in Publication
data available

Library of Congress Cataloguing in Publication
data available

ISBN 1-85230-362-X

CONTENTS

DEDICATION

To the memory of my father and the other men in
my life who have catapulted me into living and
transforming my chosen patterns of dysfunction;
and to my three children for their unflinching love
and tolerance through the storms.

Only you choose the circumstances of your life
Only you created the need for those circumstances
Only you determine your rate of development
Only you may claim your victories
Only you bear your shortcomings
Only you are responsible for you
For what you are and for who you will become

ACKNOWLEDGEMENTS

This book is unashamedly dedicated to those people who, like myself, may superficially appear to need little help, having enjoyed many material advantages; but who have also suffered the emotional and spiritual deprivation that, however well hidden, so often goes with that sort of life. Only now are we beginning to understand the enormous price paid by later generations for the patterns established by their forebears.

The solution offered to such people has all too often been along the lines of counting their blessings and getting on with life. I will try to show that only when we acknowledge and confront the vacuum at the centre of ourselves and the patterns we have inherited can we hope to take full advantage of the lighter side. Freedom must be won, whoever we are. Only then can we lead our lives to their full potential and, in the process, free our children from the destructive patterns they will otherwise inevitably inherit and pass on in their turn to the next generation.

Although this is the first page of the book, it has been written last, so that I can look back over the last few years of writing and recall all the help and kindness I have received from my family and many friends. I can only hope that what I have written may increase in some way their awareness of family patterns, to compensate them for the time and energy they have given to my quest.

First and foremost there is my publisher Michael Mann of Element Books who agreed to publish my first efforts as an author in this time of heavy recession. To those such as Georgina Gooding, Susie Rougier, Venetia Cobb, Rory Macpherson, Francis Kinsman and Morag Hood who helped so much with its construction and typing, and to my long-suffering editor Martin Noble who wrote and rewrote with such patience and insight. Lastly to all those who either told me I could not write a book, or told me that too many other people had written books on families, or that if I did write one I must do it along the lines that so-and-so had written his or hers . . . without them I would never have found the courage to do it my way.

Annie McCaffry

FOREWORD

INTERCONNECTIONS

To do justice to the theme of this book I have to involve the whole of myself, as a human being, with my own story: from my early years of feeling myself in the presence of angels, at one with their light, colour and sound; later as a teenage patient with rheumatic fever, and then rheumatoid arthritis; and as a wife and a mother, combining those roles with being a healer and psychotherapist. Latterly I have let go of all my previously learned techniques to move my understanding of life and my work into the exploration of another whole dimension. If any of these areas were to be excluded, I would be unable to cover all the ground that the subject demands.

I have therefore brought together as examples stories from my own life, case histories, and interpretations of mystical experiences. It may seem a confusing mixture to the reader looking from the outside, but, from within the journey of my life and work, it reflects the interconnection of the guiding essence of each of us – the sense of *knowing that we know* at the deeper levels of our emotional, psychological and mental selves. The all-knowing part of the self is, I feel, richer by far than all our psychological and mental systems. For me, life is about movement, and dis-ease is where we get caught up, unable to move on, in the same way that a boulder in the river prevents its easy flow.

Part I of the book concentrates more on my personal story and that of my family; Part II deals in more detail, but still in a very personal way, with different aspects of therapy, and in the final part, I develop this further and describe how I have, in a sense, gone 'beyond therapy'. By including short auto-biographical sketches of my life I have endeavoured to show

how my journey so nearly ended up on the road to incurability. My hope is that, in having challenged my own various dysfunctions and dis-ease, I may inspire at least some other sufferers with the wish to seek the way out according to their own intuition. Much has become clearer to me in hindsight which could be brought home to many millions of people suffering from dis-ease, enabling them to do something about it for themselves. I know now that there is indeed a choice.

THE NATURE OF DISEASE

There are two schools of thought as to the nature of disease. First is the old reasoning method that regards a disease such as rheumatoid arthritis as in itself incurable, but capable of being alleviated. Secondly there are those who know that dis-ease has a number of causes, all of which are capable of being released unless death is the over-riding choice. This has been my own experience and also that of others with differing diseases with whom I have worked over the past thirty years. Far from being incurable there is also every hope of eradicating the need for the repetitive patterns of such diseases within families, by understanding and untrapping what is held at a cellular level as memory within the body, which, as I now discover, manifests itself in many different ways as tumours, allergies, breathing or circulatory conditions – even deformities.

Treatment of disease today is thus being carried out by two very different schools of thought, but the doors of possibility are opening to permit people to become fully responsible. What was unconscious a few years back is fast surfacing into consciousness. Those who, like myself, have undone the knots and watched their disease and its symptoms evaporate can aspire to bring this reality to the notice of others. They, too, will then have a chance to discard their disease and the dysfunction it causes physically, mentally, emotionally and spiritually, and transform the hole in their life into the wholeness which, after all, is our birthright, if we can just dare to embrace it.

AWAKENING TO THE SELF

I have come to realize that there are mysteries of the mind and the psyche that are beyond rational proof. Some things I have already glimpsed, but each week that goes by, I understand more. I feel that every experience in my life has been part of an awakening process, and that the very nature of dis-ease can play an important part in our lives.

To find the course and purpose of my life, and know how I am living it, I have somehow had to make the time and find the place to be absolutely alone. All the answers are there inside myself, of that I am convinced, and to spend time in the silence is what has brought me to my next frontier. The process of listening reveals both the signposts and the right time to venture out again into unknown territory. I have been able to do this because I am fortunate enough to own a house in the Scottish hills where I can go and let the thoughts think through me.

Somewhere each of us has a paralyzed part of our lives, a part that feels 'dead'. From the evidence of others, and from my own experience of what I released of my own life-force at near-death, I conclude that our struggle through pain is a learning experience in bringing what is unconscious in us into consciousness. This is a fundamental part of our ongoing journey and, ultimately, of our ability to stand alone. Absolute self-honesty and courage in not separating from the experience is the key to miracle cures!

People are like stained-glass windows: their true beauty can only be seen when there is light from within. The darker the night the brighter the windows.

UNTRAPPING THE MEMORIES

Feelings that we try to deny and hide govern much of our lives by the unconscious hold they have on us. In risking surrender to them we loosen the life that has been trapped, and thus reintegrate that life within our whole being instead of being controlled by our heads for fear of experiencing the truth our bodies hold. I am now convinced that the language of the body is that of our deepest self; to discover and trust this has been a large portion of my journey and subsequent work with others. Living life fully is the symphony of the different bodies of our mind, emotions and spirit in harmony with one another, expressing themselves in the physical world.

For the past thirty years my work has been grounded in the recognition that any one aspect of a person permits access to the whole. Each of us express our inner selves in different ways, at different times, and hence each of the individual sessions I have with a client is quite different from the next. This flexibility provides an effective means of touching a wide variety of human conditions, but responsibility for change rests with the client.

Through the gentle, intuitive touch of the fingers, I can 'hear' the memories of trapped experiences. Through verbal expression and sometimes certain physical movements that allow the nervous muscular reconnection, through pictures or their feelings, the memories surface, and healing through what I would call the reorganization of energy in the person takes place. In the last few years, the manner in which I work has changed again, becoming simpler, yet more effective in a more dynamic way.

WORKING WITH MY HANDS

When I talk of working with my hands, I mean that I place my hands intuitively, each on a different area of someone's body and allow myself to drop completely into a 'listening' mode. My energy therefore focuses somewhere between my two hands. My mind is completely empty, as it might be when one sits down in front of a cinema screen awaiting the sounds and the pictures with open anticipation. Once my hands have tuned into the person's energy they 'play', in the way that the trained accomplished musician lets go of all he has learnt to become one with the music – advancing well beyond any technique. So it is with me and my hands.

MANIFESTING OUR LIFE PURPOSE

I am now ready to share the story of my life because of my deeper understanding of life and death and because of my realization of the significance not only of our early years, but also of the gestation period and the period of preparation prior to conception.

This last area, the 'unmanifest out of time', is now being explored and acknowledged, as is the acceptance of guidance and comfort that can be received from dimensions that as yet few of us perceive.

In manifesting our life purpose, I believe there are no coincidences. The parents we choose, our teachers, our friends, our relationships, all those who play parts in our lives are all pieces of a plan that eventually we can become fully aware of having chosen.

As I work with others, I see that for each of us the themes are few, the variations many. For example, I had to be virtually still-born, to lose my father, stepfather and brother, to suffer from rheumatoid arthritis at nineteen, to be abandoned by my husband with my second child on the way, to go through anorexia with one of my daughters – and many more opportunities for learning about myself – in order to awaken to my life purpose.

My early childhood loneliness and later isolation were all preparations for my life ahead. To survive my adult despair I had to know I could find my solace and strength in nature, as I did as a child. An early marriage, children, and working through years of disease and extreme emotional hardship gave me an understanding that I would never otherwise have reached.

I now realize that it is our personal choice whether we permit ourselves to continue living as victims of resentment, co-dependency or self-pity, with the need for revenge, or whether we walk through life's tragedies – and we all have them – and experience them in compassion and gentleness with ourselves as life's way of 'kneading' us into some sort of shape. In this way we become strengthened and more capable of letting go to walk on again in continued transformation.

My destiny was not to bring up my family in Scotland,

happily losing myself in the beauty of its nature, but rather to
be catapulted out of its 'womb' and to make something of the
deeply buried unconscious dysfunctional patterns on both
sides of my family. First it is a matter of understanding that we
are able to do this, and then of acting on it. To be fully present
facing our guilt and our fears, we need the courage and honesty
to look within ourselves, to identify our fears, greed, guilt and
shame – whatever prevents our true development. If we can
follow our intuition and live it, not concerning ourselves with
what others may think and say about us (what others think of
us is none of our business!) we can externalize all this, and our
self pity will be transformed into understanding, and compassion for ourselves and others. We are both teachers and students, and our rewards will come when they are least expected.

Courage is not a matter of being brave, without feeling fear,
but rather of being terrified and facing it; and again and again
walking on through it into the unknown.

In writing this book I have aimed to address those who want
more from their lives, by unfolding a deeper understanding of
their inner wisdom, and of our multi-dimensionalism. Specif-
ically I have tried to address those ready to accept disease as
dis-ease and be responsible for its transformation; to awaken
and expand people's consciousness to perceive other dimensions that can be utilized to enhance our lives in the here
and now; and to encourage people to reach out beyond their
greatest fear for the knowledge and understanding that is
hidden there and then to bring it into everyday life.

Today I understand time as 'All is now' and thus the notion
of past and future becomes meaningless. Trauma traps us in
the past, the fears of which we project into the future, hence
our perceived need to separate into past and future what is in
fact whole.

Now, as I see it, the body is the tabernacle of the soul, and
its physical structure holds all our life's memories within it. In
this discovery all our answers are fundamentally within; our
inner personal life reflects our outer, either in similarity or in
polarity.

In regaining, accepting and trusting those memories it
becomes possible to live again the laughter, lightness and the
spontaneity of the child within us.

My beliefs are that as above, so below; as within, so without. All that is around me is the faceted mirror of the many
aspects within me, and my journey is towards joy and freedom. As I have healed my own bruises within, the healing has
been reflected in my attitude to life in the world and to my
interconnections with those around me. I have journeyed
through many therapies: physical, mental, emotional and
spiritual. Letting-go, letting-go, and letting-go has been the
process; forgiving and accepting, and owning myself bit by
bit. I can now genuinely begin to feel love and gratitude for the
sponsorship that this my life and those that are around me
have provided for this journey to my self.

PART ONE

The Unconscious Ease
of the Child

ONE

MY APPROACH
TO HEALING

What is not understood is put away.
What is put away is feared.
What we fear we hate.

Before I tell you more about the journey to my self – which is
not just my story but the story of the journey we must all
make, and always have made, towards our true freedom – I
would like to say a little about my approach as a healer. I
hope this will show, at the outset, the stage I have now
reached.

In this introduction I want to present a simple view of
how I work with clients, giving a few examples to illustrate
this.

There is no single way that I commence a session. As the
person enters, I simply get a feeling as to how I will start.
However, when working with a group, be it for four days
(now I prefer not to do less), or perhaps for two weeks, I begin
each day with some of Moshe Feldenkrais's movements (see
p. 52). I use them intuitively as they come into my mind and I
have integrated them into the rest of my work as I watch the
body language in front of me. The same movement seems to
produce very different experiences in clients. One person
may react emotionally, another may come up against enormous mental control, and another may experience very little,
if anything, until later. The memory of rape when moving hips

can emerge and, in the same way, the decision to manifest cancer in a particular area of the body has surfaced during such times. These happenings provide the gateway through which the day unfolds. Each group is different, each day is different, and I believe no group forms by chance. It is simply an opportunity to journey further to ourselves.

When directing a group in Kenya I asked one of the participants for her experience of the Feldenkrais movements that we had done that morning. She said she had enjoyed it but was rather ashamed that she had felt very little. It subsequently transpired as I worked with her, her daughter and her grandchild, that through deep lack of self-worth and abandonment in childhood she had cut herself off from her feelings and, indeed, from her body. Her much loved and very beautiful daughter had a generation further on given birth to a Down's Syndrome boy with a hole in his heart. As we worked, 'granny' began to see her part in the pattern of an emotionally frozen heart that had, two generations on, resulted in the physical manifestation of her 'all-heart' little grandson – but his physical heart had a hole. Everyone adored that little boy, he had metaphorically speaking 'opened their hearts'. Today they are each owning their own pain and gradually melting it to give heart again to themselves. The mirror image worked, but at great cost. These are the kind of patterns I believe we can transform.

Most of us know that our deepest feelings are held in our gut. That which we cannot 'stomach' in childhood gets frozen, the memory numbs and, in fear lest we cannot cope with life, the fear is drawn up to lodge in the chest; the throat closes, and the head takes over control of our lives. You can try to experience this by giving yourself a fright and noticing what happens to the breath, and what happens to the fear.

Our bodies can also illustrate our connection to the earth. It is common knowledge that our fear-oriented diseases are held in the area of the chest: where we breathe from. At the first signs of stress and lack of trust in that fragile area the breath quickens to a point of hyperventilation, separating us from the body and so from the earth. In order to reconnect the body to the earth I find placing my hands on the client's legs, the body's natural support, enables him or her to reconnect with greater ease. I have dealt in more detail with associated anatomical areas in Chapter 10.

After I have tuned in to a client's level of energy, my hands automatically go to the parts of the body where the memories are ready to let go, regardless of the location of the pain. While my fingers 'listen', information about the person's life patterns comes to me, as 'mind pictures', and from these I form questions which I ask the client. The questions relate to where my hands are listening in at any one time.

This brings in the mind and its belief patterns. People want to be cured and to take responsibility for more quality in their lives, but most of us do not know how. We've forgotten how to hear the body's language and, if and when we do, all too often we judge and change the vital information that we learn. My diagnosis of a person's energy counterpart establishes the seat from which physical problems manifest, usually two years later. Very often outward symptoms of illness appear in quite different areas from the site of the congestion on the energy level. For instance, I have worked on legs and ankles when, say, the neck is completely locked. By revitalizing the energy flow, so-called incurable complaints can change and ultimately disappear, just as my own rheumatoid arthritis has. It can take up to three days, or it can work instantly, just as by unfreezing a water pipe in one area of a house, the whole system is affected and can move more freely. The body knows what to do once there is the flow of energy again.

A lot of energy is held tight in emotions and sometimes I have felt myself being asked to stand aside while an angelic level of healing intervenes.

As I will show throughout this book, I believe that freedom and joy in life come from living through the fear and pain until it gives way. In other words, trusting to the life-force's ability to transform everything that is frozen back again to light and love.

Let me clarify my findings of the different stages of the process of reconnection. I have learnt on my inner travels that therapeutic techniques play their part in helping the head to understand: through reading books and listening to the stories of others, the head can then risk connecting to the fear that the chest holds; but what I have discovered is that if we can release the mind and risk letting go further, we experience the reconnection of energy trapped in the fear. This energy, once released in the head and chest, can slip down to the stomach, and then the legs, so that a sense of physical strength can return. Particularly after severe shock of all kinds the life-force energy retreats from the body and requires the safeness to trust to live again, to be fully here and in the body. My hands provide that. Our intimate relationships do too, but only until we can stand alone. It is only when we risk ourselves 'experiencing' that we can begin to say we 'know'. It is the same with each experience in life. We get to the edge and have the choice to move through our fear and risk 'swimming' or to add to the fear already there.

It is quite often that I find myself working with my hands for two-hour sessions on legs and feet alone. I know that feelings are more easily acknowledged and expressed when there is a sense of support and safeness from the legs and feet, just as the tree depends on its roots for its stability. This also seems to create safety for the mind. If feelings are encouraged to be released before there is stability and some sense of connectedness to the ground, then instead of our integrating further with the body the very reverse happens, and we separate further from the body and become frozen in a state of no man's land. I suggest that this is what occurs in mental disease when the fear to move is so great. I have heard a client say, 'I do not know whether it is more terrifying to live or to die. I seem to be on a wire fence.' In such terror it may be impossible for the client to undo that pattern in his or her lifetime and so it will pass on to the next generation, although not always manifesting in the same way.

When I find great fear, fear that wants to jump from the body, from the room and from life, I will suggest that my client sits in a chair as opposed to lying down. This has the effect of helping them to remain more present: they can see me and my expressions, we can talk as my hands establish contact with (usually) their legs (life's support) and/or feet. They seem at once to accept my hands as an anchor. Automatically their breathing deepens as trust returns, and there is more connection to the body which they often describe as feeling heavier with much more ease and safety.

In lying on a table the client can separate himself more easily from what is taking place, absenting himself from the process and, at times, particularly of great pain or loss, this is appropriate. When sitting in a chair, on the other hand, the client is drawn into being present and this is often a better approach for those who have difficulty in finding the will to be here at all.

With no expectations from either myself or the client, the logical aspect of the mind ceases to control or judge, and experience moves in.

Here is an example. Janet's friend arrived and lay down confidently on her tummy on the table. To my surprise, within minutes she shot up again, in a state of acute panic and agitation. It was clearly an effort for her to stay in the room. Completely unconsciously I had instantly and intuitively moved to the other side of the room, giving her plenty of space. I gave her my full support to go, but as she gradually gained her composure, she said she had no idea what had happened, or what the fear was about, since it had nothing to do with being here or with me. Janet had given her all the confidence that she needed on that score. 'No, she would like to stay.'

Here I suggested that she might feel happier if we sat together and I worked on her legs and feet. She agreed, and all went well. She went home smiling, saying she felt stronger and safer. In three weeks she returned and I laughingly asked her if she would risk lying on the table. She did, and exactly the same thing happened. This time I was consciously ready for it but she got annoyed with herself for reacting in the same way, saying she could not understand what was happening. Standing well away from her, I asked her whether she would be willing, taking all the time that she needed to do so, to lie down on the table on her tummy once more, slowly and with awareness. I asked her to tell me where she thought she might be, how old she thought she was, and what might be happening.

Three minutes later she said as she lay there, 'I am four years old. I am in my bed and my mother is leaning over me saying, "If you don't be quiet and go to sleep I'll kill you." ' I, in leaning over her had brought up this memory of panic. The reality of the story was that mum's lover was there for the evening and mum did not want her little daughter calling out and disturbing them. The little four-year-old, feeling pushed to one side, was calling mum from her bedroom to get her attention. The session took the client through her panic for the last time.

From that point on I began to trust more and more my ability to work intuitively and risk going beyond techniques.

THE MAN IN THE ASH TRAY

An interesting example I encountered of someone living separated from his body was a man I worked with in Texas who had had much abuse in childhood. Although successful as a businessman, he had been in analytical therapy for twelve years when he came to me. I placed my hands on his back and, sensing his absence, asked him where he was. He replied without hesitation, 'In the ash tray on the table over there.' So taking him at his word, I simply asked if it was our work together, or whether it was that he lived his life from there. He replied that he had forgotten how it was to be in his body; he was used to living life in this separated way. Due to his early experiences of fear and pain this was his norm.

Tom had a favourite daughter whose feet were physically turned in so that she walked on the outside edges of her feet. Unable, and on some level undoubtedly unwilling, to put her feet flat on the ground, she was destined for an operation during the following weeks. Her situation demonstrated at a tangible, physical level, the father's pattern – the instep relating to the stomach and its feelings. I asked Tom if he could come into his body, if he thought that he could help his daughter's connection to the earth. After quite a struggle he said yes, he would try anything for her, though he felt he could not do it for himself.

Having made his decision it was only minutes before he was laughing at the ease and strength he felt. Being heavier made him feel more solid and safe, and ultimately he said that, had he known it would be so easy to do, he would indeed have done so years ago. His daughter never had the operation but instead worked through Moshe Feldenkrais's movements. Over a short period of months she reached her fear of no support and her ankles gradually began to straighten and her

feet flattened out on the ground. All the energy Tom was using
to resist his body was manifesting physically. The Earth is
about our mother and our feelings. He'd had his abused. It
took his daughter's feet to awaken him to the fact that he could
help change that pattern. The *idea* of facing his fear was one
hundred per cent worse than his choice to face it. Within
minutes the fear was gone. It is not, however, I must stress,
always possible for clients to face such fear willingly.

We can look into nature as a wonderful example, in the way
that trees first put their roots down into the ground to take
hold, and then the branches grow up and out to embrace the
world. Here then is our blueprint. Yet in noticing the many
times in which it is the legs and feet where I begin my work with
clients I have come to recognize how unrooted most of us are. It
is no wonder that we also feel so unsafe with our strong feelings.

I have come to understand that early trauma, which seems
to be present in all our lives to some extent, is connected with
society's beliefs about sex and birth. Possibly the most unusual
and crucial experience of trauma is that of our birth. In so
many cases, the doctors remove this natural experience from
the mother and child for no good reason, and the child, with
its own innate knowing of right timing, is instead birthed
in someone else's time. I now understand both from my own
birth experience and the work I have done, together with one
of my daughters re-explaining hers, that this creates an enormous resistance and resentment towards life and often towards
the mother too, but above all it leads to a fear of 'being taken
over by others' at a survival level. It later manifests as frozen
fear, held in the chest, thereby separating the energies in the
upper body from those in the lower; or you could say the
thinking from the feelings.

In growing up the person becomes aware of not feeling
complete, and yet because the trauma is unconsciously hidden
he does not know why, and his life becomes full of compensa-
tions. I believe that as much as 70 per cent of our life-force
energy then gets trapped in such experiences. Families' beliefs
about sex also colour and traumatize our experience of our
own conception and the months up until our birth (see Chapter 13); because of these early interferences there will be the

need, at some point, to 're-birth' ourselves in our own time in
order to alter our commitment to being here on earth. We are
talking here of the possible causal level of trauma within the
baby.

Trapped memories cause pain, and pain causes disease. In
re-living a memory as it surfaces our life-force can transform it
at a DNA or cellular level and thus free the pattern that is trapped, or we can choose early death to rest awhile, if necessary,
before gathering the tools for another shot at transformation.

There are many levels of transformation involved in breaking a pattern of three or four generations. To my knowledge
the men in my family have not, as yet, taken any part, but
fathers will often accept through their daughters what they
cannot tolerate from their wives or mothers. The change that
comes about through reconnection can, at the deepest level, be
transformation. Transformation occurs when, at the deepest
level of our being, the life-force that empowers our physical
structure lets go of parts of that structure to allow it to alter
into a completely different form, just as the caterpillar meta-
morphoses into the butterfly. The mind does not like this
letting-go process since it has no part in it, and it therefore
plays every trick and game it can to avoid arriving at this place
where it has no control.

As a society, most of us carry such huge degrees of pain and
anxiety that it is as much as we can do to read about it, listen to
others, or occasionally talk about it. Just as there is a right time
to take a cake from the oven, or for a baby to be born, so there
is a right time for each of us to become responsible in letting go
of another trapped part that leads to further wholeness with
ourselves.

People decide to make appointments with me at the time
they choose and in that way it is their inner intelligence
nudging them, not my interference and control. Synchronicity
plays an astonishing part in this: a space in my diary always
seems available even if sometimes it is due to a cancellation
or to my being available at a weekend when normally I would
not be. I believe that society can only transform as a whole by
each of us being responsible for our own inner change.

I now know the courage it takes to face – not to mention
walk through – the parts of ourselves that we separate from in

our early years, lest we fail to survive the memories of desolation and abandonment, and die. There are those, for example, who have chosen to take up positions of authority in our society while their own personal emotional lives lie in chaos. They would hope to hide this from the outside world. Our outward lives either mirror or represent the polar opposite of our inner feelings, and if the inner and outer do not reflect harmony with one another, then disease, accidents, or death will be the result.

I was able to note that as people are a part of family patterns, so are we a part of social patterns. Everywhere everyday-life is nothing more than the reflection of a society's inner journey. Social attitudes and beliefs are hard to change, in the same way that fear of personal judgement and being different keeps us inclined to stay with what we think we know rather than risk the exploration of our boundaries. Personal internal resentment and inferiority within a nation blows up into one person's control and dictatorship in an endeavour to control another country and its wealth.

At this moment of writing, I am doing pioneering work which I am excited and happy with – another stage. Until recently I have worked within one or another form of technique involving a manipulation of energy. By this I mean that I will choose the framework (technique) within which I will work so that any change within a client becomes subject to that framework. If for example I break my leg and the surgeon sets and mends it, a manipulation of energy has taken place and I am helped. At this level the cause of the break is not touched. Now when I work with someone it is not in the capacity of what helps within a technique, but rather the greatest help that can come about, on any level – by bypassing or one could say going *beyond* techniques. This is the pure life-force at work, outside any framework. It is simply life itself. Without this force any technique would not work, but the skill itself is confined within certain limits. These limits are the dimensions of time, space and matter which are created, I believe, by the human mind. I go into more detail about this in Part III.

This is the new context that I am exploring, and in all pioneering work the rules change because we enter the unknown.

What happens here that does not happen within the framework of techniques? I suspect that the energies of the destructive, dysfunctional hereditary patterns, which at present we all bring into this life with us, can be transformed at the causal level. Perhaps even the frequency of that person's energy is changed into a finer substance, nearer again to light. The memories, beliefs and accretions that stick to our cellular structure prevent such transformation and therefore prevent our manifesting as light. Our lives are lived as if through a filter. Back to mind come my early childhood experiences of oneness with light, colour and sound. Am I perhaps getting nearer to experiencing this consciously without, as before, having to leave my body to do so?

Someone described the way I work as assigning words to what is essentially a non-verbal current of energy as it charges through my hands and takes the most constructively useful way to facilitate transformation. It is like a ticker-tape intelligence, but from the heart and adding mediumistic understanding. But whereas the medium, metaphorically speaking, makes the telephone call home for you, my way encourages you to make your own. It is my sincere hope that this book will do likewise.

TWO

CHILDHOOD IN SCOTLAND –
UNCONSCIOUS EASE

I was born on 26 November 1937 at my grandparents' home at Welton near Daventry. The elder of two children, my childhood was lived between Welton and its nurseries on the top floor of that large, imposing house (I never knew it in later life as it was pulled down to form an estate of small houses surrounding the lovely lake), and Scotland, my parents' home. There, although it was wartime – during which my father died when I was four and a half years old – we never knew want of any kind in our daily lives, and seldom heard or saw anything to do with the military.

My brother and I learned to ride, tend and care for the farm animals, and to help with the dairy and berry-picking. We lived in a beautiful house, full of beautiful things, overlooking the River Tay. With so much free time to roam about we had to find our own amusements, so although we were dearly looked after by Nanny, who has also been as much part of my own children's lives, we were really very independent.

We were not a truly typically country family in that my father, who was educated at Wellington as was his father, inherited his baronetcy at a young age. Although he served as a Black Watch officer in World War II, he was ill-suited to the military, except for his humour, good looks, and wonderful ability to relate to people of all kinds. My mother was very shy, an identical twin, and the sixth daughter of a man who had hoped so much for a son. She was very beautiful but what little confidence she had in herself diminished almost entirely after my father's death, and although she did remarry when I was seventeen, this was not a very happy union for her.

During our childhood my mother lived almost a reclusive life, and after the death of my father she found solace from her devastation by creating beauty in the acres around our home. She restored the dereliction surrounding the large loch and brought back to abundance both walled gardens – and, as if that was not enough, she then created a rose garden. Needle-work in all its varieties was her forte and she and Nanny made all our clothes; she also contributed to much of the interior decoration in the house.

She seldom read a book, but she had a wonderful wisdom and humanity. As I look back on her life – her loss of her twin sister in early death, the loss of two husbands and also my brother – I realize she had very great courage to remain living at all. As my children later gave me a reason to survive, so did I and my brother offer this for my mother. She gave us a beau-tiful, warm home, even though not very many people ever came there.

DISCOVERING MY HEALING ABILITY

By the age of ten, I would spend many hours roaming through the farm buildings of the Scottish estate with their usual col-lection of stray animals. It seemed natural for me to build a safeness for them, and whether they were half-wild cats, baby ducks that had almost drowned, or a chick that the mother had sat on, I would sit with food and talk to them as any country child might. As their trust grew I would handle them and within the warmth and love of my childlike hands the weaknesses would strengthen and life return. An unspoken rapport grew up between me and these 'unfortunates' which in turn gave much needed warmth to the lonely child that I was inside.

So from early days I used my hands to heal as a natural reac-tion to 'hurt'. It was equally (and unconsciously) natural for me as a child to leave my body – was I ever in it? – and 'go home', expanding into the light and colour of all life. Those Scottish sunsets would draw me into another dimension where all was possible. It seems, looking back, that the way I work with people now is not very different from the child I then was with the animals, and although my actions and the experiences are now very conscious, it is the energy of light through my hands that is still the catalyst for transformation.

EDUCATION AND THE ONSET OF PAIN

Formal education not having been part of my mother's life was, in turn, not greatly encouraged in mine, although I was dispatched, at the age of seven, to board at my aunt's school in Northamptonshire – my first experience of structure other than Nanny's nursery. The same things would happen at the same time each day. Later my education was continued at an Anglican convent in Wantage, but at school I tended to be naughty and found it hard to learn through books. I had far too many questions that never got answered – no one, I felt, wanted to listen to me, so my solace became needlework and art and music to which I loved to dance as well as listen.

By my early teens my lower back was giving me considerable pain. This was put down to falling on the ice when skating and not referred to by anyone more than was absolutely necessary in the hope that it would disappear or was I perhaps 'making it up' to gain attention? In fact, it manifested later as rheumatoid arthritis.

I think it was here, during these adolescent years, that I began to collapse on life, feeling trapped and let down yet unable to alter the situation. One summer holiday was spent almost entirely in bed with rheumatic fever. I just grew more angry and rebellious inside, building on – I see in retrospect – the unconscious despair I had already experienced at my father's death.

I wonder now if, without my love of nature and the sense of belonging to it, I, too, might not have found remaining on earth too much to cope with. I used to watch the autumn skies, and the flight of the geese. I stared in wonder at their dark, V-shaped formation crossing the evening sky. How did they know when to fly to the sun? Who told them what season it was? The absence of people and close family life in early teens meant that my mother's lap was substituted by that of nature, my hurts being healed in that way. Although in pain, I was

learning to 'forget' it since no one was particularly interested
– and anyway disease was never allowed to be the natural
order of things; it was just a matter of getting on with something else. Boarding in the Anglican English convent gave me
little, and took away a great deal: my freedom.

I now realized that my ongoing dialogue with the many
levels of beings and life – which I had until now assumed was
something that everyone did – was suddenly gone. The English nuns decided that God and Chapel were to replace it, but
alas they did not, and I felt more alone and isolated in spite
of the crowded classroom and dormitories. I hated not having
my own room. I hated the sameness of everything and I hated
the English for being so unlike the Scots, and for being
proud of it! How could life decree that a few years later I
would marry an Englishman and make my home away from
Scotland? Looking back it now appears that my early life was
one long saga of battling alone to break the mould into which I
was born.

I did well enough at my studies. However, although no one
seemed to notice, I had great trouble with reading. I would
suddenly be unable to see the words and terror would over-
come me whenever I had to read aloud. The exposure of being
asked to speak and be listened to made me freeze. Now I
recognize this as part of my early childhood pattern of feeling
that no one heard me, or even wanted to, and, further back,
to when my mother was 4–6 weeks into her pregnancy, and
when my father was convinced that his baby (me) would be a
boy, all added to my being valueless.

Boarding school was like a prison: I was trapped; one of a
flock. I hated the noise and I hated being herded about in
someone else's time. I retreated to the art room, where there
was silence and relative space. As I had little idea of relating to
others, I had few friends, usually ringleaders and rebels, but
also few enemies; not that I think anyone noticed. Life felt
heavy: and at night I found it hard to breathe. I lived in a
vacuum, with very little motivation, unless moved by one of
the friendly ringleaders.

My endless complaining resulted in my mother's removing
me from the further influence of the nuns, and a series of
domestic science courses were arranged to make sure I was

occupied; I had no idea what I wanted, and less of how to get it. I felt heavy and fat and tired and lethargic. I was fifteen and my mother and granny said it was due to my age! I do not remember having any attitude to my body or having any conversations about 'womanly things' with anyone. Three years earlier at the age of eleven, and quite without explanation, my brother had to have his bath in another bathroom which seemed utterly bewildering. (My mother and I never had the times together that I had with my children at this age, or enjoyed the discussions and fun that come out of conversations with children discovering their bodies.)

Meanwhile I was getting less 'at ease' with myself, although I was still following the whims of society and my mother's 'oughts' and 'shoulds'. Nothing had much meaning except as a preparation for the inevitable suitable marriage of the future. School had knocked out of me my connection with life experienced through nature, somehow severing my connection to the many unseen *levels* I had lived in before. If I had any ambition that had taken over from the Pony Club, it was to continue with music and painting. Although a history of art course in Florence formed a part of my informal cultural education, on the whole these ambitions were frowned upon as frivolous. Any mention of university or a job was out of the question. Anyway, my few abilities did not seem to equip me for very much, apart from marriage. Instead the London Season was agreed to, not exactly willingly, but my mother found me a suitable chaperone, settled me in London, and duly caught the night train back to Scotland. Numb with fright – but not alone in that, as I found out – I dared to 'emerge' and a month later found myself having the most wonderful time. Whatever pain was in my back did not get worse by dancing all night and sleeping all day. The support wheels were suddenly off the bike, and I was away. I was seventeen and still entirely unconscious of my life, of being me at all! These years of fun and irresponsibility ended with one of my closest girlfriends becoming engaged to a man I had grown very attached to. Three days prior to her marriage I myself married another man in the naive hope that I could thereby numb the hurt in my heart.

THREE

UNDERSTANDING
THE FAMILY PATTERNS

Although to all outward appearances my start in life was a privileged one, it was actually very rough and deprived, and I would now like to go back to my early childhood experience, enlarging on those aspects that formed recurring patterns through several generations.

I was almost still-born, and after two and a half days of labour my mother gave birth to me – or more correctly the doctors did – a girl, instead of the longed-for son and heir. Poor Mama, how overwhelming must have been her sense of failure. She herself was after all a twin and the sixth and last daughter of parents who had been desperately hoping for a son.

My father was greatly disappointed, too. Having convinced himself and his friends that I was going to be a boy, the fact that I was a girl somehow affected his manhood.

But there I was, soon to grow into a pretty little girl of whom Daddy was wholly proud. I gave him my small and willing heart, and he gave me his. I was the centre of his world until 8 October 1938, when Robert Arthur was born. Mother and child were not well, and both needed care. Anxiety surrounded the household but no one explained why. Here, then, was already my second experience of being abandoned.

When I was nearly two, with my father preparing to leave for war and Mama unconsciously knowing he would not return, our lives were governed by Nanny and Kathie from the top-floor nurseries of my mother's childhood home at Welton. We were cozy and secure, in spite of the underlying fog of unspoken anxiety. Only Granny understood my needs and gave me the things I wanted. She died when I was in my teens, but no one asked if I would like to go to her funeral. I undoubtedly felt a deeper connection to my grandmother and Nanny than to either of my parents, and although I have a close relationship with each of my three daughters, my mother has established the same maternal closeness in their lives too.

In 1939 war was declared and we moved back to Scotland where my father rejoined his regiment. During this time my mother seemed uncertain about everything. Now she had two children and was faced with the prospect of handling her household by herself, a pattern that I too, was to find myself repeating. This was not helped by my father's premonition of the date of his death which he saw one day written across the newspaper he was reading. My mother knew of this when he left to go to war, and two years later in 1942 he was indeed dead. I was nearly five, my brother three, my mother desolate. Once more we all leaned on Nanny for support. Once more no one said anything, and no one explained. Our daily routine continued.

I think my own sense of abandonment and that of my mother dated back to my father's leaving for war, rather than his actual death. It was as if he really died for us when he left home, knowing even then that he was going to die.

I don't remember ever being told that my father was dead, or even that he would not be coming back. There was just a numb silence and a sense of deep bewilderment which I later recognized as rage. It was many years afterwards that I touched the despair and pain that I had locked away during that time and my fury that, having said 'Look after Mummie till I come back,' he had left me forever.

Innocently, in my deep love for him I had agreed to this. I would have agreed to anything. He had broken my trust, as it was to be broken many times again by the men in my life. I was forty-five before that memory, trapped in my left hip, was ready to give up its anger. 'I trusted you and you let me down,' were the words torn from me and released as my hip joint gave way under the osteopath's adept hands, the hip that had hurt since I was thirteen years old and which nothing could relieve.

Only now can I see that the 'not trusting' of my father is the pattern, the line that I carried on into my marriages. And the same grief of abandonment was to shred my life again when both my stepfather and my brother died within a year of each other.

The experiences I have drawn upon are essentially those undergone in a privileged background. It seems to me that people often look upon the 'privileged' as somewhat removed from being just human. But I hope that the example of myself and my family shows that they, too, long to follow who they feel they are and not what they are expected to be. Yet that very structure is the soul's choice.

It is interesting to notice for a moment here, how people from humble backgrounds live with an obvious uncomplicated connection to the fundamental human values of integrity, honesty and morality. In coming out of this mould, they have their fears to face in 'climbing up', but little to lose.

People from privileged backgrounds, on the other hand, live in ivory towers by a social code of 'shoulds' and 'oughts'. These belief patterns separate them from fundamental integrity with themselves. In coming out of this mould they have their fears of 'climbing down', of losing their separateness and finding their ordinariness.

Our parents play a fundamental part in all our lives until we can arrive at a place in our own development at which we have lived through what they are and integrated this into what we are. I would therefore like to give each a place here at the beginning of this book. I have learnt so much more about them both since my mother's death and what I have experienced through it.

FATHER

The wounds we experience through our fathers take a great toll on our subsequent relationships to others. My father was my first friend and, because he died and was not there to talk to, to give to or receive from, or to play with, when I grew up it was very frightening to touch, trust and be close to a man, and to form a lasting intimate relationship without any model of how to do so. What I could have learnt instinctively from my father, had he been there for me, I had to learn through the trial and error of my relationships in order to heal the wounds of being isolated merely because I did not know how to get any closer. Both of my marriages were full of not knowing how to please and interact and so, in fear of rejection, I pretended.

This father wound can gradually heal through deep close friendships of vulnerability and trust; but because of our deep unconscious memory of loss of trust, these friendships are hard to find and harder to keep. Whether our father actually dies as mine did, or is just away on business, many of us have trusted only to be let down, or become broken-hearted and abandoned. That is the child's memory, and later we fear trusting another with our heart.

Yet what else can we do but risk it? If not, we become dead, waiting around immobilized in protective armour, closed for repair! I find that imagining myself as the other person in any kind of relationship can give me some idea of how they feel, and this helps me to be more able to listen and support. After all, I have chosen them to be my mirror image to show me more of the part of myself that I cannot see.

MOTHER

Our mothers can teach us to nurture ourselves: but a mother can only teach her child to value itself if she values herself. I'm afraid that, like me, most of us do not learn this from our mothers, and our relationships to our bodies reflect it. We learn instinctively different kinds of trust and mistrust from our mothers. For instance, I was often fed not because I was hungry, but because it was a mealtime, and I was often put to sleep when I wasn't tired, and so I grew to mistrust my own internal messages. Taken to extremes this mistrust, when programmed into an adult, will make him or her uncomfortable with, or unwilling to care for, himself or herself, as in anorexia. Hopelessly, these adults endeavour to identify with everyone else and their needs, in an attempt to find them-selves. I did this at school, and later with boyfriends, losing myself in the lives of others in order to find an identity. It was no one's fault that my family, like many others, suffered this lack of nurturing which I believe can, when it becomes chronic, lead to addictive behaviour.

My mother extended her Victorian upbringing to her body; she dressed well and smiled, and thereby hid the chaos of her inner despair. The exercise she took was confined to walking or gardening. As for dancing; hunt balls and private dances were acceptable, but anything else in her view smacked of promiscuity and lack of dignity. Thus I do not remember having any positive attitude to my body as a child. I remember being fat and feeling heavy and lethargic all my school life, and for quite a while after.

From the far memory work that I have done to release my own pain, I now knew that the whole gestation period plays a very large part in our life. The patterns of joy or pain that are set up as we develop in those nine months, we continue to play out in our own lives. Given my mother's history, whatever the conscious joy at holding me as a baby in her arms after my birth, her (unconscious) thought was one of disappointment – in me, in herself, and possibly in her husband too. For myself, even in gestation, I experienced this as rejection (as did my second daughter in her gestation) and whatever the subsequent relationship between mother and child at a conscious level, that unconscious rejection still exists. Fortunately it is now possible through one of any number of therapies to bring that unconscious bruise to the surface, and to heal it.

My mother's way to survive her loss was through work. As a Taurean she chose the land and her garden, and when the Scottish winter evenings drew in, she and Nanny set about making curtains and chair covers and clothes for us. I remember her making bagpipes for my brother out of my father's kilt and an old hot water bottle, some bamboo sticks and a recorder. He would play them for hours, imitating the sound of the pipes, as my mother's sewing machine sang in the background. Mostly I hated the clothes she made me, with their frills and bows and matching knickers – since to be a boy was what really counted. It was not till many years later that I understood where that belief came from.

I do not remember ever having had much emotional contact with my mother. I think she always felt it very difficult to deal with me; the understanding and gentleness came from my maternal grandmother, and the 'getting on with life' bit from Nanny. And although there were many other people around me they made little impression.

My mother worked and smoked and lived in fear that something would happen to us. Perhaps even then my brother knew that for him it would. However, I have always been convinced of a long life ahead of me, and of the necessity of gritting my teeth to find the strength to push out into it and not allow anyone to stop me – my birth again in replay! – and my mother found this hard to handle.

Symbolically, we lived at the end of a long drive. The Rolls was there for travel, but it seldom saw the road, and the chauffeur was mostly occupied with sawing logs for the winter. Communication with the outside world was of minimal priority. If my brother and I ever did get to the end of the drive there was a bus that would stop at the gate, but travelling anywhere took so long and appeared so difficult to organize that it was easier not to go, to feel powerless and, instead, to complain. But once more, nobody heard. Years later, looking back at the cycles in my life, I could see repeats of this sensation of being trapped down the long drive as a child. At boarding school, in my first marriage, with the children, there was always the feeling and resentment of being trapped, unable to get out, taking me back to the experience of my birth.

Now I can see this as the gradual recognition of my will, and the bringing into consciousness of the deep unconscious masculine side of myself that it was my task to reclaim in this lifetime, or die as at other times I had. As my will to live gradually emerged, the choking fear came with it. There was too much yet to cope with, too much that was still unconscious, too much I did not yet understand about the fear and where it came from; except that it would choke me if I did not hold it down, and choking meant being cut off from Life. This time I had chosen to survive. The choking and terror of not surviving was, as I later discovered, the trapped trauma of my birth and pre-birth.

My mother played another most significant part in my life; a part with which I have had a titanic struggle: that it is enough to be a woman. I see, as we came closer together in her later years, that this was made possible once I let go of my judgement and resentment of her. I have grown because of the person she was, because of the acceptance of having discovered that I had chosen her, as we all choose our parents. I have grown because in her I can see my own fear, my lack of identity, my feelings of inadequacy; and in seeing them mirrored for me, I can choose, as can each of us, to keep them or to change them. I can also choose to own or to deny my own qualities (again mirrored by her) of strength and endurance, kindness, humanity, homeliness and courage. Similarly, in all three of my daughters' lives I am learning about their different choices; as I break my own boundaries, I watch them breaking theirs and feel enormously privileged to be a part of their processes.

So through my mother I have found and owned the woman in myself; and now the depth, the softness, the vulnerability and the self-honesty is available as a source of strength from which I had cut myself off before. I am conscious of the change in quality that this has brought into my life. I see how it helps the people with whom I work to touch and own these qualities in themselves; I see also how it can threaten those who are afraid to live life to the full themselves. I see how my mother's cutting herself off from the outside world has been such a key factor in my decision to stop hiding in unconscious denial and to recreate my own contact with the outside. I see how her negativity and fear has helped my resolve to confront a similar fear. I see how my change is also the change of my own children through the unseen ties that unite those linked by blood, through the electrical circuit that connects them.

If one element is strengthened, it strengthens the whole system; if one circuit cuts out, everyone in that system is affected. I hope that the day will soon come when we can all be both receivers and transmitters of the full voltage. When it does the planet itself will have changed and truly moved into a New Age.

But sometimes if one person in a relationship chooses to change or accelerate, it can send the other in the opposite direction. We each have our own speed of evolution, and must adhere to our own knowing. Resistance to change can be the expression of denial, but – choice again – it can be the time of building up courage before the leap forward. All the ingredients have to be there before the cake is baked; we cannot move forward in consciousness if we only have half of them. Times of apparent void turn out to be times of waiting for that last ingredient.

We cannot dodge the issue. We can put it off even to death; but I am firmly convinced that there is nothing in our lives that we do not choose, be it illness or death, failure or success. Nothing is by chance. On some level, albeit an unconscious one, a choice, with a reason for making it, has been made by the soul. We are wholly responsible for our lives and for what we make of them. Our journey has many levels, with the outer worldly journey always reflecting the inner spiritual one. As with everything else, balance is what we seek in living our full potential as human beings.

What is not learned instinctively as a child from our parents has to be consciously acquired later through relationships. We can blame our 'wounds' for our lives not working, or choose to heal them ourselves in order to become free.

FOUR

WAKING UP –
MY FIRST MARRIAGE

Here
We have hope of a new life when we meet –
We lose hope when we lose that person
In hopelessness we can find the un-hoped-for . . .

By my late teens the back pains were in most of my body, and I was experiencing unexpected blackouts. Two weeks after my marriage at the age of twenty-one to W.J., a young cavalry officer, I developed a new, acute and mysterious pain. I was rushed into hospital in Edinburgh where my appendix was removed. I lay there while the blue-veiled nuns looked after me, running in and out saying that I was too young to be married. Years later when I re-entered this experience it became clear that the operation had been quite unnecessary. I could hear the doctors agreeing to take the appendix out not knowing what else to do. The pain, centred above my solar plexus, had been a signal of my awakening to another level of myself and the pain coming from my diaphragm had more to do with my new life and moving out of the home and its safety than anything else.

Those around me approved of my decision to marry – and it was in accordance with the beliefs I had assimilated: nice girls learned to cook and sew and find a suitable husband. There is nothing wrong with that, of course, if it suits you. All of us begin to find our identity through relationship with someone else. I was just beginning and, as others, I needed acceptance and love in order to grow.

My understanding of life's lessons is that from early on we each develop two sides of the personality – the ego, the part that stands alone in the world as 'I', of which in my case I had no notion, and the adaptable part that can also be part of another or others respectively. In a marriage, if you learn about yourself first, you at least know what it is that you can offer another person in the union, and (just as important) what you cannot offer. I had no idea of either!

In contrast to my own experience, most young people today are choosing to know themselves first. At their age I would not ever have had the courage to step out alone; I was still caught in the net of 'what people-and-my-mother-might-think' if I did anything outside the prescribed norm. I remember very little of this actually being said in so many words, but messages were implied by looks and gestures, and reinforced in my own judgement of others, which was in reality the severe judgement of myself, of course. It never occurred to me that it might equally be praise!

By the age of twenty-two the pain and stiffness in my joints and the blackouts I was having were confirmed by a chiropractor as symptomatic of a steady progress towards rheumatoid arthritis. My mother did not seem to take this in. I now understand that in acknowledging my pain, she would have felt her own – her deep sense of failure and outrage. To stay alive, she had to remain numb to these unconscious, well-repressed feelings.

I, on the other hand, remember deciding: one, I do not want that; and two, if I know myself 100 per cent, it is logical that I can become 100 per cent fit. And as I began to awaken to my own dis-ease, I began to question the healing energy I seemed to have. If I was doing so very little which yet resulted in a great deal, what was happening? Even my small daughter could be put to sleep when I put my hands on her.

I searched for books and started my learning. Lillian Young, a radionics specialist to whom I had first been sent to treat my back pains when I was fifteen, helped me with her knowledge of diet, homoeopathy, and radionics. Well, I thought, a bit of this and a bit of that and some Yoga and I will be a 100 per cent fit in no time. That was thirty years ago, and only now can I say that I have completed the cycle of clearing my system of the arthritis and of the rheumatic fever, having tackled the emotional patterns involved, and others besides.

I have discovered how the most difficult situations always offer the profoundest lessons in our growth to future freedom. I have discovered life's ever-abundant cycles, and seen how an opportunity for choice has presented itself which at the time I have not recognized or refused to recognize. So it has re-surfaced, re-presenting itself again and again in varying forms, until eventually, through the mind's surrender, a clearer understanding has dawned and I have been ready to cut yet another tie.

But at this stage of my life I was not so much cutting ties as creating them, and the system did not help me. In Druidic times there were apparently two levels of marriage – on the more primitive level there was the coming together of two people to have a child; this union was expected to last only until the child was old enough to be integrated into the community around it, possibly at about five years of age. At the enlightened level there was the Initiates' marriage, which was for life. This involved a course of instruction by the Temple Elders and a period of engagement. Other initiates, already imbued with spiritual teachings and understanding, guided, formed and enabled this period of engagement which lasted some months before a firm decision to marry was made or not. This higher marriage, a 'Temple Union', did not take place until the couple were wholly versed in spiritual discipline and had undergone rigorous training as to the implications of those levels of union.

Today we marry with what remains of the ritual of the initiate but with the consciousness of the primitive. I feel many of us have lost the true understanding of even the word marriage. Perhaps the failure of our many marriages today will help those who follow to awaken to the spiritual aspect of this union. What some of us refer to as the New Consciousness is really the 'Old' that we are remembering, re-awakening to the wisdom of ancient times, in preparation for the New Age of Wisdom. Arthur Guirdham speaks of man's progression through the physical age on to the mental age, and now back through the age of Wisdom to oneness with all life.

This is the ideal, but it does not always seem so at the time. First marriage, for me, was far more the fact that I 'did it their way'. I was a cavalry officer's wife, going to polo matches, giving dinners. I lived in seven houses in three years, I had a lovely daughter (A.L. born on 28 May 1961) and a young nanny from Glasgow, who in the same old traditional way was dressed in navy and pushed a navy Marmet pram, with a monogrammed pram-cover. I look back on those family photographs and wonder if that was ever really me. What I created was a repetition of my own childhood, even to our living many of those years at my old home.

Although the polo matches and rowdy parties, during which my husband and his fellow officers sometimes sustained minor injuries, gave me plenty of scope for practising my healing abilities, I was not a very good officer's wife. Not that I failed to try or that I hated the life – I loved it – it was my way, to which a large part of me had been conditioned. But the rest of me had not a clue as to how to stay contained in that hopelessly structured existence. It was like school all over again. It seemed so narrow and limited and quite absurd not to have friends of all ages and ranks, including civilians – even Germans were still thought of as 'enemies'. I loved the yearly all-ranks dance with everyone having fun and dancing for the sake of dancing. The reels and the pipes reminded me again of my father.

Four years after the solemn marriage vows – after my saying with all my heart and soul, 'I give all of myself to you, for better or for worse, to have and to hold from this day forward and for ever more' and subconsciously adding 'For Heaven's sake, never give me back to myself!' – the Universe in its abundance, gave me back to myself, with no home and practically no money, despite the belief system that my husband would provide for me. My innocent vows had been squandered. I remember the humiliation, the outrage and the pain that anyone could treat *me* in that way! I had been abandoned by my husband, with my second child on the way. The Army had sent him to the Middle East where someone else's wife found him.

My second daughter, H.M.C., who was born on 5 January

1963, referred to this time in our lives much later on, admitting
that she had seriously wondered if her father had left because
she was not his daughter. My eldest daughter A.L. replied to
her, 'I've always thought that Dad might not have left if you
had not been born.' Her resentment towards her sister over all
these years seemed to stem from then, she said.

After our separation I lived for two years in the little house
next to the walled garden in the grounds of my old home. Only
accessible over a field from the home farm, it was back in the
silence of nature. Once again, the wisdom of Lillian Young
helped hold my life together. As regards any mental or emotional stress she would say, 'Work it through by using your
hands.' So my cooking and housekeeping improved a hun-
dredfold; I made bread and cakes as never before, I made
curtains and re-covered my feather eiderdown. I created a
garden from the wilderness round the cottage. I grew so
close to Nature that I knew how the sunlight, at different
times of the day, touched each tree around that little house
and transformed it. Was I re-echoing my mother, and her own
loss?

I became so much a part of the changing seasons of the year
that I felt an integral aspect of all nature. I knew the birds and
had a family of hedgehogs that I fed. The solace for my pain
was again in Nature's deafening silence which spoke to me
with so much strength and gentleness.

Without doubt, my second daughter H.M.C. brought me
great opportunities for growth and learning. I christened her
with three names, in case her father from whom I had heard
nothing since the day she was born should want to change
them. I thought I was choosing at random; yet the first name
that came upon me was that of the very woman whose attractions he had succumbed to when he had first been sent over-
seas. I certainly chose her second name, and we have used it
ever since; her third name was that of her father's ultimate and
second wife. I do not think this was coincidental and neither
does she. Once more, we are in the clutches of the family
pattern.

Our outward human journey, visible to family, friends, col-
leagues and associates, constitutes the story of our lives. At
this stage I was still absolutely unaware of the soul's learning,

the Inner Journey. My life was at a fairly primitive level of survival with two babies, my marriage shattered, and at odds with my Anglo-Catholic upbringing. If you have no visions and no calling to the Church then marriage is the next appropriate move. For me it had not worked that way.

During this time of needing to isolate myself with nature I learned more about the energy of light and thought and the astonishing beneficial effect of absent healing as practised by Harry Edwards. I had written to Harry Edwards, describing how my husband had abandoned us and wished to have no further contact with us. This was devastating for me as the unconscious 'virginal' wife who was about to give birth, knowing I had done nothing to deserve such misfortune. Back came monthly letters full of astonishingly perceptive information about the equal devastation and non-understanding my husband was experiencing in having got caught up with another woman so hopelessly in such circumstances.

How could Harry Edwards have known what was happening, with my husband in Bahrain and with no contact or verbal information given to him whatsoever? This was indeed a revelation. Not, you understand, that I could share it with my family! That would only have caused judgement and disbelief, and I badly needed something to hold on to. All I could do was to reply to Harry Edwards, giving him an update on any communication I might have had with my husband during that month. There was none.

Yet Harry Edwards, I always felt, did have a hand in the brief, transitory period in which my first husband returned to his family. The months that followed were the most desperate of my life as I slowly became aware that his only reason for returning was that the Army would have dismissed him if he had not. While he took his rage out on me, I took my despair out on him, and in the end I collapsed. Finally I put the two girls in the car and we parted forever.

At the same time as I got in touch with Harry Edwards I also became the first patient of Patricia Macmanaway, who lived with her husband, Bruce, in a village near my home in Scotland. The centre for healing they created there was still in its early days, but their work with backs in particular, as well as Bruce's dowsing skills, was becoming known. In later years the Macmanaways were to do much to make acceptable what was then considered strange and mumbo-jumbo.

Bruce had been an army officer and, as a prisoner-of-war, he began to experiment with and develop his healing abilities. It often seemed as though Patricia was in his shadow and yet she was a sensitive and fine healer herself. For the first time I began to learn about someone else's hands on me. My visits were comforting and supporting for me, and although we did not speak much, she understood. I would go home uplifted and somewhat more at ease physically with my arthritic self.

After two years of isolation, I had gained enough strength and confidence to decide to go to London, find a school for my elder child and a job for myself, and live in Kensington somewhere between Harrods and Hyde Park! So, I found my house between Harrods and the Park; the first girlfriend I met after that put me in touch with a wonderful little school run by Diana Willcox, and with no qualifications I found myself designing and making up children's clothes to support the nanny I had decided to have to help me with them.

I never felt that a punishing all-day routine with the children brought out the best in me. The lesson here was to have the courage to go ahead with what I truly felt was best for us all, and trust in life to provide (as I shook with terror). Above all, I learned not to waste time and energy justifying, but to 'walk on', as Christmas Humphreys so aptly suggests. Children create their own experiences; we as parents are only the chosen vehicles to get them here.

My first marriage ended in divorce in 1962 and was later annulled by the Catholic Church on the grounds that I did not know what I was promising at the time, so I could not be held responsible. There were three tribunals and twelve witnesses required for the annulment. I thought what they were saying was utterly ridiculous. (I then married a Catholic.) Much later, as my perception grew towards understanding the deeper significance of those promises, I realized that I promised 'as a child' in all 'faith' but with no understanding of the commitment on an initiate's level. How could I? I knew nothing of that level of myself.

Supposing 'until death do us part' meant the death of the union on an inner level. Marriages are made in heaven we hear – we are in 'heaven' when love fills our hearts. That is what I wanted.

My first marriage was from need (only I did not know it) and my needs were many, only I did not know them. We called it 'love', this attraction one for the other!

The initiate's marriage is the spiritual union of two adults, emotionally independent of one another and free from the need to depend. Generally speaking men and women who embark on marriage between the ages of twenty and thirty have not yet explored this level of themselves and for much of our society today it remains so. Even when there is an intention, we dare not risk the journey through our feelings. I survived and coped just as my mother had at my father's death – I buried the pain in my body as my background had taught me, lived for my children and never expressed emotion. I carried on as if I were in control. I was! I had rheumatoid arthritis.

The pattern had been repeated – my husband left without telling me and thereafter refused to communicate with me – just as my father had, as it had seemed to me as a young child, 'refused to communicate' after he had died. I froze in fury and despair. At least I had been rescued from up that long drive; I had made it to the world outside, and had two lovely daughters. I was also beginning to wake up.

TAKING RESPONSIBILITY FOR THIS LIFETIME

So much of what I am writing in this book is everyone's story, is everyone's struggle, but in other ways – and perhaps that is just why I write it. At times in our lives we all need an outstretched hand to haul us across the next bridge, or to wake us up to where we are on our own path. You cannot give anyone else their answers; but we can all help each other to reach them. I have generally found that to recognize where I am on my path it is helpful to take a look at the people around me and the situations which I have drawn into my life. If we have eyes to see, there is the mirror image of everything within ourselves.

The key, however, is the desire to do so. Amidst the despair and emptiness that I felt at this time, I never lost the will to carry on. I began taking Alexander Technique lessons with

Irene Tasker to help ease the pain in my back. Aged eighty-three, a friend and colleague of Dr Margery Blackie, the inspiring homoeopath, she had trained with Alexander himself.

My body was causing me excruciating pain and stiffness, my lower back was constantly collapsing, I was terrified at being alone with two small children and my liver developed hepatitis. I have since experienced the anger I carried in that organ.

The doctor sent me home to bed for two weeks; not a very practical solution with two small children to feed and look after. So, instead of going to bed, I crawled on to a train to Ross-on-Wye, where Lillian Young squeezed and pressed, mostly on my back – as she put it 'unblocking the drains' connected with the anger, the pain and the despair that I was carrying – after which she tucked me into bed with a suitable homoeopathic remedy, lots of books and lots of herbal teas.

Less than forty-eight hours later, having slept almost continuously, except when undergoing another session of barbaric treatment, I woke with a streaming cold. My system was once again flowing and so were the emotions, and I returned to my family quite able to continue with life and work. Now, I genuinely began to want to understand the deeper significance of Life. I look back today to that time and see that my days were so full of fear that sleep became a way of escape, shutting my eyes as my way of not being responsible, not able-to-respond. Years later in work on my past lives with Lynn Buess (see p. 119), and with Ilana Rhubenfeld in New York (see p. 51), I began to understand this terror that shook my body and choked my breath at a level I could not seem to probe at that earlier time.

This is what I was experiencing: my mother's momentary but desperate disappointment at my birth that I was a girl, and my father's equal disappointment that as such I could not inherit his title, not to mention that he had told everyone I was going to be a boy. None of this lasted, I hasten to add, and was probably never a conscious thought for either of them. But for me that memory implanted itself so early that I carried the black burden of unconscious anger and resentment, particularly towards my mother, until 1980 when I began to recognize her family pattern and re-experience the time from my conception.

As I have related, she was the youngest and sixth daughter of a family with no sons. She had a twin sister who by the age of fifteen was an alcoholic. A generation back, I found that my grandmother, although she had a brother, had faced great pain, as all the women in my family seem to have done. Little wonder, then, at my mother's immediate disappointment and feeling of failure at producing me as her first child. When you actually re-remember and touch your own early experiences like this, it makes for a clearer understanding of what really happened, which is surprisingly different from what you assumed or had been told took place. After that, it is far easier to accept life as you are living it today, and to begin to understand why it was that you chose to come to earth at this particular time and as this particular person.

This time I chose to come back as a girl – to break the matriarchal pattern. In my father's family, all the males of the past four generations have died young; my father and my brother both dying as the result of accidents at about the same age, apparently aware that it would happen, and yet unaware consciously that they had the choice that it need not.

In the years during which I trained with Ilana Rhubenfeld (see p. 51), and before that in personal intuitive sessions with Lynn Buess (see p. 119), I have been back in memory and released experiences trapped in time, but which reflected themselves now. In two previous lifetimes in particular, I died rather than take responsibility for myself and my life, just as I am tested now. In both cases I experienced my life as a man with the very same parents. I have also experienced choosing my parents and the dramatic effects that this realization had on my attitude within these relationships. I have experienced my fury with myself and my dislike of this life here on earth, its heaviness and its struggle, but I also know that this time I am conscious enough to clear the drains that are still blocked, and strong enough to carry through to fruition what I have chosen to do.

Until very recently, fear has had a lot to do with my resistance. My rheumatoid arthritis was an outward physical manifestation of all that I did not want to own. The image that I have is of a Shetland pony that puts all four little feet on the ground as if in cement, refusing to move, however coaxed, in any direction. I will not go forward. And where do we find 'will', but in the spinal column? Pain and rigidity here affects the whole body.

The back of my neck, the tightness of which was causing my headaches and blackouts at this time, is the control point for the mind over the body. As I began to acknowledge my feelings and to trust my body again, my neck and shoulders softened. My body began to feel the legs (support on the earth) as the mind let go of its control, so that it was no longer necessary to walk around three-quarters out of my body for fear that if I once descended and touched earth, I could not float out again when I needed to.

Peter Russell gave a lovely example in a lecture once, of how we can live life as if holding tightly to a rope suspended from the heavens for security. After five years of hard work, he says, at last the initiation occurs and we think we're home and dry – 'Enlightenment' – I've made it! And one finger lets go! Another seven years undergoing all sorts of trials, and the next finger lets go and so on, until we are hanging on by one finger, terrified out of our wits about survival. But at last we do finally let go, only to find that we have been standing on the ground all the time. We do not have to hold on: Life will support us, we are part of the Earth – so risk it!

It is interesting to note here that after twenty-five years of Alexander Technique work, I still return for lessons. When I started with Irene Tasker it was about sheer survival, anything to relieve the physical pain I carried. It then took about two years of having a lesson each week to bring me to a point of not needing two hours' sleep afterwards. Nowadays, though, I go back to check out and affirm in my physical body what has already been 'let go' because of the healing I have done on deeper levels. Today, I have an awareness and understanding of the patterns carried in different areas of the body, and can help people change them and release their pain.

Since then, I have also worked with Moshe Feldenkrais's remarkable sequence of movements that bring a still deeper awareness of how we hold memories in the muscles and tissues of the body, until we are ready to let them go by becoming conscious of a particular memory trapped within our own family history (see p. 52). At this stage we have a choice to see the pattern. Healing comes in allowing the release of the energy held in any one place, in the form of feelings. On release this trapped, frozen energy integrates with our life force. It is like unblocking a drain: the flow of life increases.

We are the products of influences seen and unseen – ideals, cultures and beliefs. Life is always a process of clearing to go forward, then once again consolidating and clearing to go forward. It is impossible to go forward carrying three generations of family troubles on your shoulders, and yet that very same family will have given you traditions that go way back in time and hold as good today as they ever did. We have to discriminate in our personal lives in the same way that we do in our work or business lives. What fails to work has to be cleared away to make room for what does work, so that Life becomes an ongoing creative process rather than a static, frozen, joyless existence. We each have to take the responsibility of creating this within ourselves; thus the waves of Life and joy ripple out from us and touch everyone around us.

So in these years of taking responsibility alone, both financially and emotionally, for my daughters and myself, I learned how despair can push you through fear to activity, to take responsibility for doing something. When I said, 'I can't cope,' it usually meant that I did not want to be able to. However, I found that there was always help available when I looked for it and was willing to receive it. So often we will not allow this as patterns of unworthiness creep in to our minds. In order to give, we have also to be able to receive – the one is the polarity of the other. For most of us it is easier to give, since in order to receive we have to feel worthy to be given to, and so often we do not.

RADIONICS: CHOOSING BETWEEN LIFE AND DEATH

At this time I struck up a deep and lasting respect for radionics. Today I still call up the same practitioner, Enid Eden, who for twenty-five years has been such a wonderful support in my life; nowadays I also do so in connection with some of my own clients, with whom the two of us then form a triangle. Radionics can be of enormous help on many levels. For the three

weeks during which my brother was lying in a coma before he
died at the age of thirty-five (he had been knocked down in
Edinburgh by a car which then dragged him along the road by
his coat; he suffered severe injuries to his head and legs), the
radionics instrument could give readings relating his condition
and for two days after the intensive care machines had been
switched off. It helped us to know how he was feeling while he
was trying to decide between life and death. With that knowledge I found it easier to direct my thoughts to the support of
what he was going through on his level; and at the same time
to help my mother to understand what she was experiencing at
her own human level.

It was our radionics practitioner, Enid Eden, who, when my
second daughter kept having great throat trouble, asked what
happened ante-natally that could have caused so much shock
to her, naming the month in which my then husband had left
us. Since then radionics has been a partner in helping the
children with earache; rescuing the pony when it choked on
cattle-cake; realigning the aura of a tractor-driver suffering
from severe back pain, which has never since returned;
helping a friend with a leg wound that simply would not heal
because of deep-seated emotional stress; as well as my brother's accident and death and my own endless string of dis-ease.

Today, through Dr Valerie Hunt's research in the U.S., it is
known that the body's chemistry remains the same up until
three days after death. Our minds are still fully functioning,
even though the brain is not operating during surgery or in
coma. So to talk to someone in a coma is like talking to someone who can still hear, but cannot answer because the electrical current has short-circuited.

How long it is possible to remain in that state of non-
connection I do not know – possibly till a choice is made
between life and death. In such cases, my Dutch friend Kojsha
Kemper uses muscle testing with a surrogate family member to
determine how best to create safety for the return from coma
of a sick patient. They can hear, even if to begin with there is
no apparent response. To choose life entails coming back into
the body and resuming responsibility; to choose death
involves choosing to give responsibility a miss until the next
time round. Choosing death gives us a chance to re-assess – an

opportunity to come to peace again before tackling further strife. My own experiences in memory into past lives tell me that what is not finished has to be faced again, at some time in the future, and dealt with, whether it is to do with relationships or situations. The Universe, the infinite, is not bound to our concept of time. Perhaps we can only make changes within ourselves by experiencing them 'in time', and perhaps time holds us only as long as we need to heal and integrate that individual part.

Dr Hunt has also tested the effects of various other influences on our energy fields. Thus we become debilitated, she says, when we watch television, because it is transmitting disturbed energy. Synthetic clothes, chemical bleaches, soap powders all lower our energy too. It might interest the reader that she also says that low frequency energy people (that is, those with slowed-down metabolism who are heavy in emotions and limbs) contract bacterial conditions, while higher energy people (more mentally oriented) contract viral diseases.

In contrast, we are beginning to rediscover the immensity of the mind's capabilities. We play Gregorian chants to lift the mind's vibration, to touch the Divine. If the mind-field is heightened enough, we can tune into and read each other's thoughts or have a 'Divine' experience.

Goethe says: 'The moment one definitely commits oneself, then Providence moves all. All manner of unforeseen things occur to help one that never otherwise would have occurred.'

FIVE

REMARRIAGE,
RELIEF AND REVOLT

The Colour Black: changed the consciousness of death in the West to being a destroyer of life – not an integral part of it.

Is my contact with others any more than a contact with my reflection?

In 1963, by the time I was twenty-six, I had moved back to London again and I had taken a job – my first – designing children's clothes. A few years later I had remarried, moved back to the country and, still later on, opened an art gallery which doubled up as a venue for yoga classes and public talks on such subjects as colour therapy, radionics, zone therapy and diet. A year later, I found myself taking over the yoga classes and also running the clinic started by Joe Corvo's visits to my home.

Joe began his career as a jazz musician with Dizzy Gillespie. His father was a north-country miner, his mother was a medium, and he grew up with these polarized influences. I met him after my brother died, when his zone therapy helped me to keep my system in some sort of balance as I faced the shock. Since that time Joe has helped many famous people to further well-being. He is undoubtedly an extraordinarily gifted healer from whom I have learnt a great deal, and who was the catalyst for my embarking on a 'professional' healing career. He has made a record called *Regain the Joy of Living* which, as he said, was not intended for the semi-converted like me, but for the ordinary person who had never heard of an alternative way to look at disease.

I was constantly on the telephone to Joe for his instructions. Although my hands produced results, I had little idea of what I was doing, except that I was using my intuition through them, trusting that all would be well – and it was. This was an exciting period of my life, both in my work and my new marriage. Little did I realize what lay ahead.

What do you do when you meet someone and a voice in your ear says: 'You'll marry this one, you'll wait and it will be hard work'? That is what happened. In 1967, after four-and-a-half years of ecclesiastical litigation, the Catholic Church in its wisdom annulled my first marriage in spite of my two strapping children. Was this perhaps their understanding of the two levels of marriage? I married my second husband, but mistook the nature of the hard work involved. I had everything this time that I didn't have last time in the shape of a beautiful home, both in London and in the country; a successful and doting husband, and added to this my third daughter, S.C., arrived in 1968 to join my two little girls from my previous marriage. I can remember thinking, 'Yes, this is it. I now have all I want and someone else is polishing the floors, so no "hard work".'

Probably the most significant thing that I learned in this period was that Annie was not going to get it her way and that the hard work had started. 'Life' kept intervening with alternative plans, testing my ability to cope on a human level. I would set up courses and the Nanny would leave. I knew I would travel, so obviously it was with this husband whose business took him to many parts of the world; but no, I almost always got left behind. Everything rolled me back into the home, until one day in a fury, I screamed (to no one in particular) 'All right – I will stay here – I will let go of trying to control – I will accept what is.' In that minute I saw a door open in my mind and I heard, 'When the time is right for you, you will not have to go out; people will come.' These invisible gates seemed to open on to the world. After all this struggle against the old feeling of being trapped which I had experienced at school, it gave me such a fright that I made no outside contacts for a week.

Meanwhile, a few years into the relationship all I knew was that I was allowing myself to get squashed further and further into a boneless jelly, until I began to believe that that was what I really was: incapable of anything – a hopeless cook, mother, lover, wife – plain, dreary, a complete failure. My second marriage was disintegrating during a period in which A.P. was spending much more time in London, where he was achieving considerable success materially. When he was home, he was tired and disinterested in my life, which, following my previous experiences of abandonment, I unconsciously interpreted as 'disinterested in me'.

Up came the panic: I imagined all kinds of misdemeanours on his part and when he denied these it somehow only made the panic worse. He agreed we'd move to London so that we could live more of our lives together, but it never happened.

It was then that I decided I would rather go on alone than live in the permanent state of panic that I was being abandoned again, and that my husband was not hearing my plight. Here was the repeated pattern of the past, but still not conscious. All I was conscious of was a panic bordering on hysteria, of fearing I could not cope with life for much longer. I was really on the edge and the only way to survive this was to take hold of the reins and control everything. (Was this not what my second daughter did in the near future with the onslaught of anorexia?)

I woke one morning, seven years after A.P. and I had got married, and knew that this was it: I either had to end the marriage or end up in a mental home, though if I had known what lay further ahead, a mental home might have been a happy release.

WALKING ON – WALKING OUT
INTO THE WORLD

I thought I had known fear, until I faced it now. Once again, frozen panic came at the thought of being responsible for my life; yet here I was, breaking out of the pattern I had chosen.

Rather than claim his identity, I feel my father had died to avoid the expectations of women.

The inner arguments began again. The watery woman in me was wringing her hands and whining. 'I can't do it alone, without support.' The sergeant-major was shouting, 'Travel to all corners of the earth – take up every opportunity for expansion, and prove to yourself that you can walk on alone this time.' The spoilt child was screaming, 'My way, not Thy way – I want control!' And, amid the uproar, when I could listen, there was the wise woman within myself who said, 'Go, risk, dare – but be gentle with yourself too. Know your limits, nurture yourself, attend to your needs.' It is only as you know yourself and give to yourself, that you can know others and give to them. Always listen. Don't be afraid to say no. Discriminate. Life is ebb and flow – giving out and taking in. If you travel and work and give out to others, remember always that the retreat back into the silence, the solitude, the break after the work is also part of the process. It is not a holiday separate from it, but a time to rest, listen, consolidate and gather momentum. This is a time to receive consciously from Nature, receive from those whom you have drawn around you, be nourished and allow the mirror to reflect this particular chapter of your Book of Life. See if any alterations are necessary, be with yourself, and be your own friend.

So I travelled, I risked, and again my lower back collapsed and the hips seized up. I had to throw myself on to the aeroplanes without giving myself time to think. (The hips represent our 'preparation for action' and the lower back holds fearful memories of not coping on this earthly level.) Yet every fear faced is a fear walked through. The trick is to stop and be completely in the moment, and then ask if there is fear. The thought of travelling alone would choke me at night when I would wake in a cold sweat. Yet I knew I would do it. Whatever fear I made contact with inside, as long as I ended up listening to the wise woman within me, I had confidence that all would be well. However difficult, I just had to keep walking on.

It is good to reward one's achievements. I have always found it helps to find a treat-time to give to that part of myself that has risked and dared. On my travels I rewarded myself with days off for fun and visiting, strolling in lovely places, and doing crazy child-like things, such as my snap decision to go riding through Madrid on the back of a motor-bike. What a sight I must have looked, encased in my tartan shawl, as I clutched on to the dashing young Spaniard with eyelashes that reached to Granada and thick, dark, curly hair that streamed in the wind. How much I looked forward to hearing the (loving) groans of my children at the thought of their mother making such an exhibition of herself – though of course, in truth, as I assured them, I don't suppose that anyone noticed me!

So the panic, the fear that caught my throat as if to choke me, gradually began to let go over the next two years. I really began to have the confidence that if it felt right to be somewhere, then I would be there and so would the work; and so would the money to cover my travels. Spain was an example of this, when I risked giving a weekend workshop for nothing, to prove that the law of abundance does operate where there is right thinking and right action. We all worked together with this principle, and with what had happened to prosperity in our own lives. What the workshop showed was that those attending came from all over the world and had in common a lack of identity and no sense of belonging, which were reflected in the absence of power in their lives. Money is power – very few of them had much, and if they did, they could not believe that they had. So we came to understand how we felt about having no power, how we felt about having no money, how we felt about our identity and our self-esteem. If we can change this belief into feeling that we do deserve, then we open the doors to the law of abundance. The workshop turned out to be a perfect reflection of this principle in action. At the end of the day they donated what they wanted, and in total it amounted to the normal asking price.

I was not divorced again until 1982, by which time I had moved back to London. The years between were filled with such colossal fears that, but for my children, I might have put an end to my life. This must have been the same as my mother's reaction at my father's death. Although I didn't resort to drink or drugs, I did, however, succumb to the attractions of

the third man in my life, M.C. – and with that, the decision
that I would get to know myself, for better or worse, instead of
relying as I had done on my two husbands for any form of
identity.

EXPLORING THE WILDERNESS OF ONESELF

Freedom is giving into restrictions and, arriving at that giving-
up point, exploring the wilderness of oneself. Then Life can
begin to flow more freely through us. Perhaps this is the meaning of 'Thy Will be done' – not mine, but Thine – or rather,
not Annie's but the true 'knowing' of the essence within myself, that little spark of Infinity. Getting the controlling mind
out of the way, the 'I' or ego of the personality, allows the
expression of that all-knowing part of the self.

A Bulgarian couple, who were to become my dear friends,
told me, 'If life under suppression does not kill you, it makes
you mighty strong!' and there is much truth to that. I was in
Bulgaria meeting people involved in building bridges, through
the media of arts and music for young people, to make
exchanges and form friendships. This was under the auspices
of an organization called The Spirit of Europe Foundation, initially launched by Harley Miller and the Findhorn Foundation
of Forres, Scotland.

The next years were a long and bitter struggle to obtain my
freedom and divorce, seven years later! What happened to the
arthritis in this time? I had discovered that I could heal the
physical level until I got emotionally upset, and then the pain
returned. It was something of a blow to have to accept just how
much anger and pain I was experiencing emotionally, since for
some time I had been going to weekend seminars on psychology and listening to everyone else's experiences, hoping I
would not be noticed. Now, the more I listened, the more I
realized that my experiences were just like the rest of them.

Lionel Fifield, in a lecture in England on 'Prosperity and the
Law of Abundance', made a lovely point on how so much of
our life is spent in looking at others, as if in a goldfish bowl –
criticizing, judging, gossiping – until one day we wake up and
realize, 'Hey! I'm one of them too!'

Now as I look back on the years of unravelling I have completed – freeing myself from beliefs that didn't work, attitudes that came from a lack of self-esteem, pains that I had carried since before I was born, anger at choosing to be born anyway, at my father leaving, at being a girl when boys got the attention, at having to cope alone, at being left on my own – I am led to the conclusion that this emotional level is what we all shelve. We want to run a mile from the pain and frustration of earlier years, from meeting the deprived child that we each carry within us, and yet who keeps running so loyally after us!

I have realized that there are ways of letting that energy go and transforming it in gentle ways ('less is more', as Ilana Rhubenfeld taught me), and much of my work is now involved in helping people to do just that. You cannot reach joy if pain is in the way, there has to be space for the joy and peace to emerge; we need to empty ourselves of all the anger we can, in order to allow love. Recently I spent a morning talking about anger and its effects with a group in Spain, and by lunch-time almost everyone there had a physical pain in their body. It seems to me that we fear the explosion of all the emotion we have kept for years under lock and key; and that fear of losing control and falling to pieces makes us turn the key another time in the lock.

From my experience I know that the thought is always more alarming than the action; there has never been any feeling of being out of control in any of the deep trauma work I have done with myself or anyone else. In contrast, the laughter and lightness that such a letting-go and healing can induce is truly creative.

There are many variations but few basic themes when working in this way; people are the same the world over. Different races and religions may produce different reactions – more guilt, or less freedom for women, or whatever – but in the end we are all back to working with the Masculine and Feminine principles modelled by our parents.

So my marrying again had not let me hand over the reins of my life. Seven years later I simply reached the same hurdle that I had run away from unconsciously by remarrying. That is how I see it now as I look back on the recurring cycles and opportunities that my life has offered since, but which were invisible at the time. Certainly there were moments when I heard my inner voice, but chose something else and pretended not to hear. I heard, all right – and so the Universe in its abundance brought me face to face with being alone again!

As for the 'hard work': it was hard work taking myself in hand, and never had I faced harder outward tests in order to wake me up. Even harder ones were necessary and were yet to come.

This second marriage all but annihilated my self esteem. I had felt trapped in my home, as I had at school and indeed in my whole human form – but I had learned acceptance and surrender, which freed me to move forward and take further responsibility for my own life. He had some wonderfully endearing qualities, this Irish Gemini, and his chaos taught me so well how to use time constructively when waiting. He was an intelligent and very amusing companion who was kind and generous to us all. I do not think he ever thought I would leave him and indeed neither did I. Had he been able to acknowledge my needs, as I continually asked him to do, I believe I could have forgiven him the rest, but finally I could not accept his unconscious denial of the value of my having needs that were not a part of his belief system, and which he could not tolerate.

The anguish of having to leave this man who trusted me – and in his way I am sure he loved me too – was with me for many years; as was his cruel resentment towards me for getting a divorce, and it took many more years to achieve any form of reconciliation. I think we both feared deeply that we would destroy each other emotionally. He would jump in his car and drive away to avoid issues, leaving me abandoned to my fears and with no communication (just as my father had). I am also a conscious witness of how he has transferred to our daughter the responsibility for his life and well-being which I refused to carry. I wish I could have done better, yet, without his willing co-operation, I do not think I could. I know I hurt him very deeply.

Some marriages end up like therapy sessions and work becomes merely a way of making a living instead of being a challenge and an offering to the society in which we live. As puberty is the time to find out what you have to give, so maturity is our time to give it; to give to others what you uniquely have to give while still looking to your own needs. Maturity is the culmination of all we have learnt, the time of the soul – the last lap. Few of us make it – we get stuck as I did on the journey. Birth gives us a body, childhood the heart, schooldays our mind, and lastly comes the cycle of the soul, the time when who we are and what we do become one and the same, living and manifesting it all. That is the time to make the initiates' marriage, time to commit to something – to go all the way. We can hopefully drop our games, our masks and enter a relationship with trust and loyalty, find our friend in our lover who walks us ever deeper into ourselves.

SIX

TECHNIQUES AND
BEYOND TECHNIQUES

My second marriage was over and I still felt myself to be
without a role, I felt I needed to accomplish a course of training and prove to myself that I could earn a certificate and label
myself if necessary. (Having got both three years later, in fact I
have never used either.)

As people began to confide their problems to me I realized I
had no logical knowledge on which to base my answers. I had
risked in a childlike fashion and it worked, but that was not
enough. So, leaving my two young children in my mother's
care, I flew to Virginia, USA, to Paul Solomon's Mysteries
School. This was Paul's first teacher training intensive course
and also the first of its kind, unique at the time for its multi-
levelled coverage and in its exploration of the fundamentals of
mystical understanding. What pearls of wisdom I listened to
in those weeks. We explored the understanding behind such
issues as the interlinking of our belief system with the emotions, and family structures were learnt through family sculp-
ture. Bit by bit the patterns that I found myself so locked into,
and so unaware of, emerged.

I remember special diets, little sleep, meditation classes that
included 'seeing' into a patient's system and recognizing the
areas of disease. We lived our mystical lessons in a thousand
ways. I began to see more of life than I had ever dreamed. Paul
stirred my deepest wisdom: I had never suspected that I would
be able to see into people as he was teaching us to do.

There were three people in particular – a doctor from
Nevada, a psychologist from Dallas, Texas, and a very wise
business woman from Australia – whose continuing friendship

and complementary knowledge still remain an integral part of my life's work.

It was a happy and rich few weeks in that lovely corner of America and possibly the first time I had been in the company of others of similar experience and vocation who did not find my view of life unusual. An amusing and illuminating thing happened at the end of this intensive training period. We were asked to lecture to the staff who, as well as giving so much of their time, wisdom and care, had advised us on how to engage with groups, how to use a microphone and how to present ourselves in a lecture situation. The whole thing was recorded on video, and my talk on 'How emotions manifest in our body posture' was delivered with such strident enthusiasm that I disconnected myself from the microphone. When the video was played back there were charismatic actions but no voice!

BECOMING AWARE OF TECHNIQUES

On arrival home I was surprised to hear the relief in my mother's voice that I was safe; she had envisaged me incarcerated in some religious sect that might demand my total alliance. She feared for my sanity. After my return I think she feared for her own, in that life for me had taken on a new and different perspective. Up until then my childhood, marriage, gallery and subsequent clinic had been as a pre-training, establishing my trust in instinct; but on my return it was time for logical and correlating techniques. Subsequently I have been able to return to using my instinct and intuition, having integrated the logical learning of techniques into the greater whole.

Roberto Assagioli's work on parapsychology was becoming known, as was Gestalt therapy, and a man whose work I was later to be much influenced by was Moshe Feldenkrais. Once home I read avidly all I could lay my hands on, sending my children to rest after lunch to make more space in which to do so. My healing work continued as and when people came, which to my surprise they did. I began to go to weekend conferences to learn more. The first Mystics and Scientists Conference at Winchester, put on by the Wrekin Trust, was an exciting event in the way it brought these two different worlds together.

I began to take Alexander Technique lessons again. The pain in my body had grown considerably worse once more. I was becoming much more conscious of its causes, but the stress caused by the fear that I might not be able to cope alone was pushing me to find further answers. The hypertension under which I was living my life resulted in a 35-minute lesson knocking me out, so that I was compelled to sleep for two hours to recover. This brought me back in touch with my body again and re-established my stability. From this point on anything I learned through undoing my own dis-ease I risked incorporating into what was beginning to emerge as 'Annie's way of working with others'.

In my mid-forties, with all three daughters at boarding school, I took what was for me the gigantic risk of committing myself to a three-year training with Ilana Rhubenfeld at her School of Synergy in New York from 1983 to 1985. What I learnt in these next few years constitutes the basis of my work today.

Ilana Rhubenfeld began her professional life as a musical conductor, but finding herself with back pain she began taking Alexander Technique lessons. After a time she found these lessons bringing to the surface deep feelings which her teacher, instead of welcoming, said would have to be dealt with by another sort of therapist.

Eventually Ilana decided to combine the Alexander Technique with other therapies that would allow these feelings to be re-integrated into the self. She opened her own school in New York and was the first person to present such therapy in the (then) USSR and Brazil. I met her in England after she had added Moshe Feldenkrais's movements to the synergy training.

'I can teach you what I know,' she'd say. 'Take it and use it and each of you add what is already yours.' This was a beautiful way to teach, and it was an inspiration to watch the results as she worked. I feel most fortunate to have been her student for those three intensive years.

Every morning we would have a two-hour class of Feldenkrais's movements so that we could experience through our own bodies and know what connected to what. Then we worked with our hands on each other as emotional issues

surfaced as a result of the movements. In the afternoon Ilana
would demonstrate different applications of her techniques
either on one of us, or on some handicapped client of hers, or
perhaps she would have us watch the automatically synchron-
ized movements of a baby. This enabled us to see for ourselves, and so understand, the best coordination of movement.
Later in the day we would discuss this. In between we ate and
played and made new friends or patched up the broken areas
of the day before.

Ilana's sensitive, intuitive and wise guidance taught us to be
aware of our own bodies through the Alexander Technique as
we worked through the synergy on others. 'You cannot release
the tension in the shoulder of another if your own shoulder is
locked,' Ilana would say. To test the sensitivity of our hands
and intuition she would lie on the massage table with her eyes
closed and we would in turn each stand behind her head and,
placing our hands very gently on either side of her head, we
would wait, trembling. 'Let go your left knee, Annie,' I can
hear her saying. How could she possibly know, lying there
with her eyes closed, what my left knee was up to? Today the
tables have turned and I too have developed that same sensitivity and ability to 'see' without my eyes, yet how it used to
frighten and bewilder us students then in 1983.

To the Alexander Technique she added Gestalt therapy.
While acknowledging Ilana's intuition and skillful use of
Gestalt therapy in her work, I could never integrate its mental
approach within my own, and I have tended to use the more
intuitive method of far memory or past-life journeys as some
call it, in its place. She also added the four thousand or more
movements, so brilliantly and intuitively discovered and used
by Moshe Feldenkrais.

Moshe worked with cerebral palsy and other paralysis to
bring back to life what was frozen in a moment in time. He left
behind a legacy of brilliance for those ready to trust to instinct.
We were taught to by-pass the reasons and the labels and to
re-enter with the client the original experience as it emerged
through listening with our hands; following them intuitively,
we learnt that any expectations usually proved wrong and
always limited the work. Nothing ever turned out as it
appeared to be going to. By placing the hands and allowing the

release everywhere but where the pain was, the pain let go.

Metaphors which would reveal deep-seated family patterns were for ever showing themselves. For example a client feeling cold, and getting colder to a point of shivering with teeth chattering, could be facing an earlier near-death experience.

My way since then has been to journey with the healing potential within the client, allowing my energy and that of the client to merge under my hands. In this way unaccountable, massive changes can come about. Less always seems to produce more. So, could it therefore be that we are allowing a certain de-crystallizing of the lenses covering the light of our true selves, as Gaston St Pierre often refers to in describing his work through the Metamorphic Technique (see p. 89)?

'Allow the person's innate intelligence to direct the session and follow it, facilitate and listen,' Ilana would say to us. 'The change will happen, you do not have to "do" to anyone.'

SEVEN

LEARNING TO TRUST

Any gaps in our early development fundamentally affect our personal relationships, no matter how strong, and so we leave, or divorce. More often than we realize, sexual immaturity, repression and guilt can make people feel desperately isolated and 'different' from their friends. Inexperienced, and scared of admitting their feelings for fear of rejection, they end up isolated and cynical, able only to create superficial or blaming relationships. Sexual energy goes into work, and is suppressed with alcohol and drugs, or is denied in the name of lust and therefore for not being wholesome. Belated puberty breeds the playboy idea. 'Open' marriages, divorces and competition between children and parents become the norm.

I left my second marriage under deep emotional strain, knowing that otherwise I would go insane from listening to and buying into all the things I was labelled as. So I had decided I would find out what I was for myself, instead of taking other people's word for it. Well, that was a surprise! I was good, I was capable, I was loving, I was wanted for all the qualities I'd been led to believe I lacked. This was so healing, so freeing, such fun. I could laugh again and play again and live spontaneously again – I came *alive*.

At last I realized that we can only truly express what we feel, not what we think we feel; and that thinking is only the idea, not the reality. But in order to find this at forty and with three children growing up, to find the child in me and live it, meant really owning that I was lovable – and that took some owning. It was a perpetual argument going on inside me day and night between the adult me and the part that said I counted for nothing and always had: fat and plain; feeling alone; not fitting in at school; wanting to paint or to dance and not being allowed to; seeing her best friend marry the man she loved.

Gradually I began to accept that part of myself, helped by the other part which said that if the desire was strong enough and true enough, if I could begin to accept and love what I had judged in myself all these years, there would be a coming together instead of a polarizing. Instead of half my energy being burned up in suppressing what I feared might come to the surface, it could be freed into living, with no judgement or rejection.

In this, my helper, my friend, my mother, at times my father, and above all my lover, was M.C., a man with whom I shared the next few years of learning. I learned that I did not always have to fight for recognition; that I could be understood; that he wanted to listen to me, not to judge me. I began to trust again, to open up and trust again.

Ready to explore the pattern in my psyche that was behind this disease, I remembered feeling the unbelievable pain from the pit of my stomach as I listened to him saying 'I will never leave you' and for the first time heard it on two levels. But I started living consciously, watching what life was giving me, understanding the significance of my opportunity, and giving full permission to myself to have it. He did the same with his life, and we grew in both stature and wisdom.

We laughed, cried, played, loved and talked with honesty, supporting each other. This was relating as I had never known it with the men in either of my marriages. I began to acknowledge my own worth and identity. Later, through working with Lynn Buess with far memory on past patterns (see Chapter 14), I saw patterns of weakness and shame that I had carried, certainly for three lifetimes before, when I had killed myself rather than claim responsibility for this masculine identity and for my purpose in life – the place of leadership that I could never take.

In the unravelling of my own life, and now in my role as a catalyst for other people's, it has been my experience that the true power to achieve comes from first of all claiming the woman within. Going down and down to the depths of one's being – either as a man or woman – and listening to that part of oneself, trusting it and recognizing its power, so rooted in the earth, allows the stability and sureness for the journey up again and out into the world. Trees are only as strong and stable as their roots. Man is the same.

In the context of relationships, woman is capable of literally woo(ing) man down to his depth, to feel and trust his innerness. Man can draw woman's inner knowingness up and out, so that she can know (in her mind) that which she knows (in her intuition). When I first married at twenty-one my belief was that without a man I was only half a person. In my second marriage at twenty-nine I knew I was not even half a person. Now I was exploring!

With the huge shifts we are now making in the process of self-understanding, no wonder there is so much fear and mistrust. Till now, we have looked back to find the rule book for our way forward; now all the outside props we have leaned on and felt certain about suddenly do not have the same value. We are having to let go of them, and trust from inside ourselves, discovering the simple wisdom which, since ancient times, we have grown away from.

Likewise we are retuning our bodies like vehicles to accommodate the changing, quickening energies that are entering our planet; allowing us once again the forgotten use of such faculties as far memory, telepathy, and non-verbal communication. As we become more attuned to 'knowing' each other through sensing, language becomes less important. 'The body never lies' – all that we are is there to be seen by those with this growing perception.

In retrospect I can see that at all times in my life I have had the opportunity to be led by my inner voice, and the times I initially did not listen were the times my mind interfered in order to get my own way. At those times in this particular relationship when we decided we would marry, it was as if I could see a pair of hands move in between us and force us apart. Yet as long as we kept these rules, and lived physically apart (although emotionally together) life offered unforetold joy and opportunities for our mutual growth and happiness. But then one day, while I was weeding the flower border I felt a hand touch my shoulder and the words 'It's time to move on now' appeared from nowhere. It seemed unbelievable after these happy years. I was stunned, yet I knew there could be no arguing. Inside I froze as I once more 'prepared to act' (repeating, as we all do, my birth experience once again).

Another phase to be faced, but how? How to move on from this, and from all we had shared and built together on many levels? So, the pain of letting go began again, of giving up, of moving on, of trusting in that voice; though as yet I was unable to explain why. I did not do it well; there was human pain in it for both of us, coupled with the nostalgia of what could have been. The insight and the lasting friendship resulted from our continued effort to make it so. What gentle gratitude I feel for the confidence and trust in myself that this relationship established.

Today M.C. is living out a whole part of his life's experience that I could not give him; while I, for the first time in my life, began to claim my own power and my worldly identity. My work began to establish itself strongly, both in England and in other parts of the world to which I travelled in subsequent years to facilitate seminars, workshops, and individual work.

On one of my trips to Kenya I had an introduction and meeting with the spiritual leader of the Boran tribe of Africa, who live on the Ethiopian border. He spoke in parable but his wisdom and message were very simple, and on many levels simultaneously we had a most absorbing discussion for some two hours via an interpreter. He wore his grass skirt and I wore my pearls yet there we were speaking as if we had known each other for ever. We talked of changes that would, in years to come, affect us equally although very differently from our very different cultures. What a privilege and unforgettable experience this was. I am now invited to the sandal-throwing ceremony with his tribe on my next visit, to which I am looking forward. They look into the future, by reading the marks of the sand made by the sandal!

EIGHT

NEAR DEATH
FOR THE LAST TIME

'He who finds his soul (in another) shall lose it. He who loses his soul for my sake [who lets go, trusting life to transform it into something more] shall find it.' What we find is 'more' of the totality of ourselves.

My relationship with M.A., then a highly successful family division barrister, was an entirely new world for me. His incisive talent was encased in a distant reserve, his will and his sensitivity compelling him to keep people at a distance until he was sure he could meet them on his own terms. Nonsense left him cold. He listened well, but heard nothing he did not want to hear; he spoke firmly and repeated what it was he wanted to say. His right to deafness was not given to his audience either in or out of court – his precision and concentration were the foundations of his mastery. He had very definite views about people, their behaviour, and the course he would follow in all that he did. By and large his patience was unrufflable; his manners were studied and he had a remote dignity that I loved. His aloof courtesy was guarded by an impenetrable reserve that barred almost all intimacy; yet I have never known a relationship more intimate.

He wooed me in every way known to man, and won me with all that was beautiful in life. My home was filled with flowers and fruit from his garden. He gave me pretty clothes and wonderful presents. For my birthday he had designed and made for me a seal, encrusted with my family crest, as if somehow he was giving me back my right to own my worldly inheritance, whereas hitherto I had maintained the image of a girl, having very little value. (As my mother must have had expectations towards my father, did I too, then, unconsciously have the same expectations of this man?)

He nurtured and supported me with such warmth and closeness that I felt I now had the right to receive it all.

Very cautiously I opened my heart to his love and generosity and in return gave in full measure my own. Yet his was a solitary heart, fearful of trusting and fearful of losing all he had fought for. He loved and guarded goodness and justice, yet he found it almost impossible to give to himself. He was ruthless and cold when threatened by the unknown; his sensitive, thin-lipped mouth would become tense and pursed, demonstrating the anguish his duties and the life he had chosen imposed on him. All else was numbed into non-existence.

I knew him for about seven years, first as a newly appointed Queen's Counsel, where a huge leather-topped desk divided him from his clients, and the mirror image reflected what must have been there for him, as he listened behind it in safety, summing up and delivering his counsel. Before we parted he was appointed a judge.

Dressed for court, this highly eccentric barrister, his pockets containing the fallen-off buttons that the endless safety pins replaced, was well thought of by the judges and on occasions he took great risks. At home on his farm he was every bit the tweedy, eccentric squire, dearly loved by me and the locals alike. Our companionship – the walks, the talks, the log fires, the garden and the peace – was a warm complementary delight, closely shared.

How I esteemed and loved so dearly this unusual yet controlled and calculating man – how much joy and intimacy we shared. I would listen to him evaluate in his own particular way the cases he had to read for that week. With his brilliance, wisdom and farsightedness he would answer my questions of what I had not fully understood about my life, in the same manner with which he summed up in Court.

'When I feel that I have no strength to go further,' he would say, 'you are there to encourage and console me. You help me feel human.'

What was happening in reality was that I was giving my

heart as completely and unconditionally now, this 'last time',
as I had done to my father. The acute abandonment by M.A.
in the present was as great as my father's death had been in the
past. The same degree of commitment of love was there and so
was the subsequent loss resulting in the re-experience of that
depth of grief, shame, fury and abandonment, with the terror
that I would not be able to survive it.

My life would have remained on tack had he been able to
wean me gently. If he could have, he would have, I am sure. It
would have helped my struggle with death so greatly to know
that I was not cut of as with my father's and my brother's
deaths, unable to say what I needed to, to be heard, and to
hear him. My loneliness was unbearable. In reasoning I knew
that the depth of my conscious pain was the depth of his
unconscious pain (as in my second marriage). In his childhood
that he seldom spoke of lay the pain which had caused his
dis-ease on a heavy scale.

I know now how it must have felt for him who had striven
so hard and who, having found me, had committed himself to
love and marriage with me and a new home. How devastating
then for him to find the terror of trusting and fear of losing
returning so unexpectedly. How great must have been his
disbelief and bewilderment at what was happening when he
loved so sincerely. And yet he was unable to recognize that he
was repeating the pattern of his childhood which had resulted
in dis-ease, so caught was he in terror, as I had been in my
second marriage. Feelings too strong to feel had been long
suppressed and denied in an attempt to survive the isolation of
his man's heart. In our heartfelt love they had been touched
once more; the closeness from which he had been cut off in
childhood, as well as the feeling of belonging to something
greater than himself. The risk of possible loss again created too
much fear in him.

I remember his stern and desperate resolve to abandon me.
When in doubt, denial is best, he said. I remember my shock
and disbelief, as I shot out of my body to somewhere on the
ceiling, hearing only the words 'last time' from somewhere
deep inside me.

Everything was suddenly gone. My life in that moment

crumbled in the disbelief of my betrayal. My past returned
again. I was once more abandoned and alone.

'You must think of this as a death,' he said. He did not know
what he said, or indeed what he was asking of me! This is what
I wrote in my shock:

My loss seems so great it is uncontainable.
My loneliness and despair so huge it freezes me from going
anywhere.
My bewilderment so overwhelming I cannot utter a sound.
My rage has gone now but it choked me till I wanted to be sick.
I long for the warmth the closeness the trust and oneness I had,
I feel raped of friendship and trust in another human. All that was
beauty has turned into self destruction, dishevelled, hate, catch-
ing what is beautiful and losing it – again – again falling –
falling – alone – my heart it will break from grief – why the
weakness, the indifference to me, the helplessness, hopelessness.
My words are not heard, my feelings are not felt or respected –
nothing – nothing again and again – back to the beginning –
another beginning – the pain – my heart – where is my strength
to go on – my legs shake – my body trembles – my mind seems
numb – only my pen writes with ease – what to make of it –
how to bear it but I will – I will again come through – the last
time – like a baby – with nothing – to start again – be born.

Some days later, at the suggestion of my dear and trusted
friend, Rosie Rawcliffe, I re-read this passage as if I had just
been born, and was thus able to realize how, in deciding to
abandon me (in order to survive his colossal fear of his own
childhood abandonment), he had catapulted me to relive at a
tangible and physical level what I had experienced in those
first few moments of my birth; when I had been abandoned
and left to die, and had had my first taste of being here,
without being recognized or valued.

Indeed I thought I would die, the pain in my heart was so
intense I could only breathe in gasps – I felt totally powerless,
and unbelievably alone, just as I did at birth – freezing the
pain and anger and disconnecting them as I had to, to survive
being still-born. Now, with M.A. and this present situation,
I was re-membering and thus dying. But this time, because I
could consciously watch the process it was dying to a part of
myself that had been frozen in near-death. In undoing this, I

did not have to die physically, as my father, brother and stepfather had chosen to do in their re-experience of that same frozen part of themselves.

So deeply did the Judge fear that his gentle, loving heart, so used and abused in the childhood of which he seldom spoke, might be broken by me that withdrawal and denial were preferable to risk. We both suffered heartbreak: he pushed his further in; I played mine out. I could neither stand, be still, nor eat, and I could not prevent the flow of tears as I gasped for breath. Curiously enough, though, between bouts such as these I could work! I was not in my body and seldom aware of it. With rheumatoid arthritis there was a constant, creeping-all-over pain. But now it was as though a dagger were in the back of my heart. The rest of me was like a jelly, melting fast!

Had this relationship not seemed to me to have the potential of being so complete, my reaction to his rejection might have been milder: instead it turned into something that threatened my life. And yet, this utter devastation that rips apart our lives is what we make fun of in society, and pretend is nothing. Seldom do we think even to stand by each other in our decision to leave a relationship, or to keep the communication going until the other can stand again. Hence where there is no healing, it often becomes impossible for the wound to heal enough ever to trust further intimacy. This, then, is surely abuse of the type I have both inflicted and received and which I will never give to myself or another again. No wonder people become addicts in order to separate themselves from this sort of despair.

Once again, trapped in my loneliness, I returned to Scotland, to the hills with their acceptance, stillness and sense of forever. This is where I went to, to feel their ageless wisdom and somehow endeavour to touch my own. In solitude, with the wind blowing me through my chaos, beyond my limits, I abandoned myself to my grief – to see what would happen. I felt the rain mingle with my tears, softly, gently on my face (I could have filled Loch Ness) or sometimes its strong and hard, astringent sting, always cleansing and refreshing. The wind seemed to carry away my grief as it did the tears from my face.

Scotland was where I last remember my father, Scotland

was the Judge's love too, from where he had so often written to me. So I would find myself driving to the same hill which he had walked on and loved and written to me about in sheer ecstasy of the experience, alone with himself. I was being called back to where I knew he had known happiness. Here I was in this very place, suddenly realizing that I was also the little girl searching in her despair and loss for her Daddy, knowing that already he had gone, as my husband-to-be had gone. Even as she walked she knew it was useless, yet something inside her drove her on, searching somewhere – he must be there. I was like Ophelia, half-lost in a desperation to find or die, half-knowing that it was only part of the process of integrating again that which had died when my father died and reinforced by the other close deaths brought to light in this present abandonment.

First there was the feeling of disbelief, then the shock and despair that catapulted me to this gateway in myself. Nothing seemed real any more. Even to cry had no meaning because the pain was beyond it. Lifeless like Ophelia I existed, sometimes here, sometimes not, drifting like a wraith, month after month, so frail, so vulnerable. Probably no one in the everyday world noticed anything except the deadness of my eyes. The days came and went; the therapy sessions came and went. The nights were torture, waking as I did to find myself almost separated from my body, hanging on by a thread as I began to hyperventilate. Radionics worked overtime on my willingness to survive this last death, as I repeated over and over, 'I can't, it's too much on my own.'

Quite consciously I had to sit up in bed at night and with an act of will commit myself to staying here. By placing my hands on my body where I felt the pain and breathlessness, I discovered that it helped me to affirm the reconnection with life in a tangible way. The drifting created a feeling of isolation from my fellow humans, of being alien and different. To be touched might have dispersed me like a cloud of dust.

I exist and I don't exist. Who am I? No answers any more. No rules to follow. Everything is different. Every molecule in my cellular system. To return it will take as long as it takes, but can I do it at all? The experience begins to transform how I perceive Life. The intention to stay has been made, but one wrong move

*on the tightrope between life and death could change my decision
and the decision governs all.*

*To be here or not to be here? To take the intermission break
just to get out of being responsible to Life and the transformation
process? No, we are here to transform ourselves to a state of
'Heaven on Earth', realizing the light that we are. Planetary consciousness is now pushing us to awaken. The Buddha's wisdom
showed us understanding of the Laws; the Christ showed us how
to love, and put them into practice. Now it is time for each one
of us to bring this universal understanding into manifestation
through the love of the heart, and to live that fact out in our own
lives.*

It was hard for me to recognize that this was no dress
rehearsal, I was on stage – NOW – it was happening now!
Vulnerability leads to listening in the deepest sense and to
having to let go, trusting to the wilderness of knowing nothing; to giving attention to that in each moment. This was all I
could do. Breathe each minute at a time to remain on earth.

*Yes, but what is this fury, this outrage, this fierce, seething anger
that the vulnerability is giving way to? That also is fact. What are
these flames from nowhere consuming the depths of my being?
Destruction, mindless fury at being here at all, at having to be
responsible for myself, at having to face this again. It is as if
I have tried for ever and achieved – what? My spine seems limp
without strength. No strength to stand alone. I'm only a woman.
Where is my Prince? cries the Cinderella in me, to give me
support. That deep, deep-seated belief that he will carry me,
save me from carrying myself. But that is not the place in my
story I am at any more. The outward princes have been there,
now it is the inward Prince I seek, the male that is me, locked and
hidden away in anger and dependency each lifetime, surfacing to
become himself and instead being drowned in 'I can't'.*

*Like nausea it sweeps through my body, consuming, breaking
through, burning my legs, my thighs, my throat . . . Pain, fury,
rage, despair at the betrayal. Shame at not being enough. Diving
into the abyss I go – risking the bottom – for the last time:
underneath all else I know this. The message from within.*

*I hate the men that have played their part in my life in bringing
me to this point of being responsible, because I always believed
that they would do it for me; I hate the women for their part in
manipulating the men I have loved into unconsciousness; I hate
my hopelessness, helplessness, loss of control, pointlessness in*

*striving on to all this rightness and truth when I am drowning in a
sea of humans pretending, acting out centre stage games of false
identity leading to nothingness, just to avoid what is inevitable.*

*And I realize that I am like them too, fighting for recognition,
bringing unconsciousness into the light. The anger is forcing all
my old belief patterns to crumble as it explodes. It also provides
the energy to move forward.*

In this search for the marriage of body and soul in solitude and
our inner darkness we find the Godself, and a need is born that
transforms our loneliness and feeling of separation into a need
to return in search of what has not been found in solitude. Our
oneness with humanity. Within the dark, still night of the soul
a child is conceived, a new experience is born, a love is ready
to express again in service to mankind.

As we become closer to the oneness of all life, I feel we
also paradoxically become more alone. This aloneness is not
loneliness, since it stems from a choice not a need. A peace
is born. Life becomes lighter and freer, and so much more
honest!

There really seems to be no need to search for what we are.
The searching is the mind's game to separate from being it. We
identify with the past in order to feel we have accomplished
something – the self image of who we are. We imprison ourselves in our past, and so distort how we perceive ourselves
now, causing a separation between who we think we are (the
past), and who we really are (the present). This uses up energy
which could be being used to attend to and live in the moment.
The fears of the past, projected into the future, create the separation that can lead to dis-ease. But the action of giving attention to the present produces its own energy and is endless and
boundless. Now was my chance to live it.

When there is complete attention right inside – not imposed,
not directed, not willed (as Krishnamurti said) then the whole
structure is alive not in the usual sense but in a different sense.
Then there is a transformation that manifests itself in the physical. I think it is a direction of death and death is that.

This is how I felt as I began to make the return journey from
the dread in near-death, fully conscious of my choice to
remain with it until 'Life' broke through and transformed
that particular pattern. Can it be that myself and my three

daughters, being women, have somehow together made conscious, and broken, a family's dysfunctional patterns in a way that can release the men in their and future generations to rebuild the family's identity in a different way?

Is my work with the present Royal Family but an echo of my ancestor's position as physician of the Royal Household in 1700?

NINE

JOURNEY
TO MY SELF

We are here to be human – not perfect.
                                    GOETHE

Here began an intense inner journey through the wilderness of
myself. Nights of feeling my body full of bubbling oil, moving, pulsing from my chest to my thighs, the rhythm of my
breath changing and in waves of energy the inner dance would
begin. My feeling would move on the breath from frozen
dread somewhere down in my groin to connect to my throat,
at the same time as feeling stuck across my middle back. Time,
acceptance of the process, trust, the frozen dread melted and
by degrees evaporated through my breathing. Each episode
had a beginning, a middle and an end. At times there was a
feeling of such intense despair that it was very nearly too
much, this transformation back to light. My legs shook and
trembled and I dreamt as if delirious at nights and woke crying: 'No, no, this can't be happening, I can't, I can't.' My mind
saw pictures of experiences and life depicted with a whole
other reality of understanding. People who had been part of
my life, alive and dead, came and went, representing images
of an aspect of my journey. Alone. Human and not a bit
perfect.
    Disease – no, Dis-ease – yes. Am I experiencing what is
called madness I wonder? But no, there is a balance. Yet the
intensity quickens within. I had not chosen death even though
I came close to it.

Society cannot deal with those who 'can't cope'; disease gets approval and/or sympathy, certainly attention. Death the same. Sheer hard work to convert what would be dis-ease into ease is received with blank looks, but this time I was strong enough to go back through the relationship of today, through the same repeat shock of abandonment and betrayal, to each situation where there was safety in being loved. Never, never again, I hear myself say, will I do this to myself – yet how to muster the strength to live?

The opportunity to help each other is there in our relationships. More often we manage to diffuse the issue or separate from it, but seldom do we help each other walk it, this journey to ourselves. The task is to live it, in order to transform slowly and steadily what starts as a basic fear of survival. As catalysts, relationships do well to bring us face to face with that which we hoped never to know about, let alone face! I dare go so far as to say that many marriages are made between desperate people, in the hope that they will not find themselves – if they live enough for the other, that is. Many of us remain in the emotional consciousness of students, unable or unwilling to grow up emotionally or spiritually.

This time, in being the one that was 'left behind', I was the one that was catapulted forward, opened up in the betrayal, given the opportunity to make the sacrifice, to give up, to let go and move on to another cycle, or to get bogged down in bitterness and blame.

The partner that runs away once again crystallizes the trauma for another cycle, unless he or she has first healed what was within the existing relationship. We can, but most of us do not. We are too ashamed and feel unnecessarily guilty or fear being trapped. I now understood how walking out of my second marriage had devastated my husband. What children we were emotionally, and how unconscious, alas.

To live in the present we must heal the past, and we will therefore tend to live in the past to the same extent that we are unreleased from it. We repeat the patterns by recreating our past in the present, in our houses, in our dress, in our chosen places of holiday and so on, repeating what to us is safe and familiar. (Of course it may be familiar, but safe, no; life keeps giving us another chance to challenge the unconscious, until in the end we can recognize what is really happening and begin then to take charge.)

My commitment was so total, his rejection so final, my shock so great that it blew open all the bygone memories of being left, repeatedly since birth. My left hip seized again. My lower back collapsed. I trusted the man I was to marry, as I had trusted the two I did marry, I trusted my brother to look after my mother, my father to look after us all, and no one was left, no one. I felt outrage, the child's blind outrage, against all the men whom I had thus trusted and who had 'let me down', against God, against life, and yet I also knew it to be a gift, a gift that if I could live the despair and keep breathing, come through the grief, allow the re-experience of being almost dead, consciously, then I would be breaking patterns on a cellular genetic level for my family and myself, transforming my entire being and loosening the structure for them.

Much of what I experienced nightly was at around 4–5 am, the same hours as before my birth. I would wake and the energy dance within my body would begin, it would last up to two hours and when completed I would fall asleep exhausted, but in peace. There seem to have been many levels acting out simultaneously but inter-connectedly. It is difficult to relate this experience of the body's energies reorganizing themselves in words, but I can say that I was gradually getting stronger, from the core of my being in a way I had not known before.

I feel that in the course of transformation I have re-experienced each of the family's diseases in energy – for example the crystallization of my mind in rheumatoid arthritis; my feeling that if I go on alone I cannot cope; the intense despair and rage of abandonment; anorexia and the denial of Life linked closely with cancer, as manifested by my daughter and mother; my not wanting to make the effort to stay alive; my feelings of worthlessness manifesting in a small growth in my right groin. This, too, disappeared later but it was important not to encourage fear of any kind if I was to live through this and out the other side. I was holding on by a gossamer thread to life on Earth.

Each time a memory came, a picture from the past, a feeling, I pinpointed it in my body where I felt it. The things that related to my growth were all attached to my worldly identity, in some way to my left shoulder, the heart's despair, and to shame and disgrace for my very existence and the fear that I had no strength to change it.

My right leg held my worldly identity. My right groin the attitudes relating to my first preparation for action in the world. So I had prepared, I had chosen with my mind and my heart and then – wham. Permission to live? Life cut off by both parents' unconscious rejection of me at birth, my mother's terror of her long labour having trapped my willingness into a feeling of 'What's the point in struggling to live?'

Our fathers equal our relatedness to the outside world. If our father is absent, we grow up with no way of knowing who we are in relationship to others. We blindly relate and so draw partners who in themselves cannot relate. Sooner or later one opts out and chooses denial or cynicism or understanding.

My growth took one year to work through. I did it alone and then, when I knew I had walked through the pain and shame, I had what remained removed. But those who have their lumps and bumps removed *before* dealing with the underlying cause still retain the unfinished business. They often build further on to the trauma and remove the opportunity to heal the cause by burying it. Surgery is separation and, like the ostrich, what I don't want to see isn't there, but alas it involves denial again! This way the pain is pushed back into unconsciousness, where it grows stronger, but will rise up again, perhaps not in the same form and perhaps not in the same generation, but it *won't go away*. I believe some 70 per cent of our being is unconscious and although we think we live from the conscious part of ourselves, it is but a game to cover up what waits, trapped in our unconscious, lifetime after lifetime, for recognition and freedom through love and self-acceptance.

Not being afraid of my own inner chaos, and not having anyone to force me into accepting disease with its labels, has allowed me to live through my fears consciously, all the way to the bottom, without controlling or denying the life within. In no way could I have done this without the primary support of Enid Eden and of radionics, with its ability to be with me on any level – even up to three days after my death if I chose! I had witnessed this in my brother's coma.

I never knew my father's father who died of TB yet at a deep, unconscious level I could see that I had drawn this weakness to me through my second husband and through the Judge (who had TB as a young man) until I could free my own unconscious chest, and thereby alter my connection to life. This unconscious 'TB' with its black anger around the heart, has been the hardest to clear of all. Waking in the night, breathing to 'go out', and having to wake myself up and affirm my decision to stay here. These same feelings of imploded anger and terror are deeply rooted in those with cancer/TB/ anorexia and the outrage as in *ME* and arthritis. Early shock separates us from the physical and although we appear to be here we are really not.

I like the way Reshad Feild says the only purpose of being here, is to be here, yet a very small percentage of us ever get here. Now I know why! Time and time again we choose to separate from, rather than join with, the experience that releases us. Through 'dying' we reach life. In mystical law, both conception and birth are seen as deaths, since they are a separation from our oneness. Our journey to ourselves, then, will take us back through our birth and gestation experience, to return again into the here and now, in order to remember what has been left behind. This undoubtedly makes us ultimately conscious of our choice in dis-ease.

The work of self knowledge requires us to listen, but for most of us our listening has become impaired to such an extent that when we do hear ourselves at the deepest level, the logical mind takes over in judgement and annihilates the message.

Until we can empty the mind of all its chatter, old beliefs and ideals, we cannot 'see' what is there. The work of self-knowledge is to 'know thyself' and as I know myself so shall I know another.

I feel that each life-cycle has its main catalyst and its teaching. At each stage life provides us with essential experiences and truths. Life itself, the living of it, what we make of the living of it through its different stages, is the path to our enlightenment. But first we have to wake up to our 'deadness'. Then there is no need to fight life, to resist it or control it; we simply surrender to it watchfully. Is that fearful?? For most of us it is, yes, very!

I found that my sadness helped the desperation of living
with my loss. Sadness releases. It hurts because it involves
'letting go' of what one is attached to. The whole of my face
and body seemed to feel droopy, my eyes looked heavy and
tired, my mouth seemed to turn down. Lines appeared on my
face that had never before been visible, (they vanished soon
afterwards), my arms hung down, my shoulders sagged and
my feet dragged, and I sighed a very great deal! Sadness makes
us act like a wilting plant, so naturally we fight it mightily! We
want to be happy and the idea we have of how to achieve it is
to avoid sadness. Yet by accepting inevitable sadness, despair,
abandonment, betrayal, however it comes, and by walking
through the 'vale of tears', we can transform that emotion into
peace and joy. True joy unfolds within the heart once sadness
has cried itself out and connected us to the core of our vulnerability and the primal attachments that constitute the 'web' of
our experience. Joy unfolds out of the emptiness.

My sadness through my tears allowed me to melt my rigidity. It shook to the core my security and stability with the
inevitability of another letting go of the handrail and moving
on to change and growth. It was another death to another
dysfunctional aspect of myself. In avoiding sadness we express
a superficial happiness, which can, at best, mask depression
and anger. As Henry Thoreau said, 'The mass of men lead
lives of quiet desperation' masking their fear, anger and sadness in the hopes that no one can see it. These are the emotions
that again and again return to haunt our lives and pass on to
our children, until we give up fleeing from them. Our challenge I feel is to accept our inescapable vulnerability and
embrace our humaneness as a necessary part of our experiencing life on earth.

Due to man's constant forging ahead, our fear of our past,
even to pretending our childhood was one of joy when so
often it was not (except on the surface), and due to our belief of
'how to behave', we punish ourselves in the present because of
hurts in the past. It takes time to dissolve fear of hurt; alternatively we can choose to be its victim and believe that life is
against us instead of for us. *A Course in Miracles* states that all
dis-ease comes from a state of unforgiveness. I would also say
that states of unforgiveness can come from pride, and from a

fear of 'what people will think if . . .' This is also caught up with our need to control a situation or someone (as if we could!).

It can be said that those that hurt, hurt others, so we should remember that when we hurt the most, so does that other person. Maybe it is only to the extent that we have felt and healed our own hurt, that we can understand and forgive those that have hurt us, sadly not always simultaneously. To me it is important to put to right a hurt I have unconsciously caused, if I can. How the other person receives that and reacts is not always favourable since we like another to carry the burden of the unsatisfactory-ness of our lives.

I believe that my mother grounded me long enough for me to make the family pattern conscious with the help of my three daughters, and so set them and their generation free. It took the women in my family to break a pattern of no identity so as to allow the boys (who took no part) to build again that identity. My mother did likewise after she died. I could feel her closely, but on another level.

When you know for yourself the journey through anger, fear and pain, then you can empathize with another. To feel compassion must be the ultimate feeling that unites and merges us with others.

You can genuinely empathize with another's fear when your own fear is clear and not confused. Compassion wears whatever 'cloak' is appropriate to the moment and uses whatever tool is necessary to get to the next place. As teachers or leaders of the way, it is our mission to lead people to freedom, not just to say that everything is going to be all right. Sometimes it is even appropriate not to go along with what is happening.

We are surrounded not only by false compassion in the form of sentimentality, but also hard-heartedness, with people having to numb their feelings to others because they are themselves so wounded and unable to respond. This is our society.

Our emotional energy needs to flow and be used if it is not to become dried out. Damming it up only causes damage to ourselves which can ultimately become suicidal. I have seen people buttoned-up like emotional corpses, speaking in monosyllables through tightly clenched teeth, eyes straight ahead. Families have different emotions that are OK to express, and others that are not. To know these things in a personal relationship is vital; the fact that we do not exchange this sort of information is one of the reasons our relating to one another becomes fragmented and dysfunctional. Clots of repression and denial set in, and our creative life-building energy is used up in avoidance.

If love is the healthy functioning of our whole emotional system, then when we love naturally it will be right and so will the whole of our interchange with ourselves and others. I believe this to be one of the prime functions that we are here on earth to demonstrate. All the world loves a lover, but hardly any of us learn how to become one!

Full of laughter and song, our bodies in movement and dance take us to joy in the heart, which deserves to relate to both God and Man.

He who believes in me (me Universal) though he die (intermission) yet shall he live (still alive in still life) and whosoever lives and believes in me shall have everlasting life and never die.

PART TWO

Dis-ease and Therapy

From a certain point onwards there is no turning back. When there is nothing to do within one's understanding, one risks what cannot be understood.

(FRANZ KAFKA)

TEN

AWAKENING TO DIS-EASE WHERE IT IS HELD IN THE BODY

BODY, MIND AND SOUL

If we trace it back to its Greek derivation, the phrase we use so often, 'I am deeply in love' really means 'I am inwardly beloved of my soul'. I think it is worth pondering on this before reading this chapter on therapy (the word 'therapy' comes from the Greek *therapia*, meaning the work of the gods; while the word 'soul' means total potency). At best therapy can only bring us to a greater understanding of experience; and, on the level of our emotional 'attachments', from being deeply in love with another to being beloved of my soul – a lover of myself on the level of soul or essence.

Verbal therapies and analyses can get stuck in the head, but can indeed assist us in arriving at the powerful door of the emotions. Their problem is that they may call us back, before we can go through the experience, lest we 'lose control'; whereas body-orientated therapies miss out the analysis, and thereby can slip into the error of acting out the feeling without ever really integrating what it was about. There are put-together synergies that aim at body-mind, which is indeed a step further, and then there is 'beyond techniques' – causal or soul therapy one could call it – where the practitioner acts simply as a catalyst for transformation to take place. This does not always happen during a session, but can take place at whatever level the client is ready for.

At the same time as my outward learning experiences with people such as Paul Solomon, Irene Tasker, Ilana Rhubenfeld, and other types of learning involving radionics, colour and sound, there was an energy-intensifying inner journey due to the fast-emerging consciousness, and my decision to risk exploration in all its forms where they presented themselves.

I had now realized that these dysfunctions and traumas I read about were not only those of other people, but possibly mine as well. I could no longer cling to society's norms and cover my inadequacies, for fear of shame and disgrace in being different. These were in the way of my life and, especially in Ilana's work and training, I found a perfect opportunity to find out more in safe circumstances.

MIND/BODY SYNERGY

Our culture teaches us to deny our feelings and our hearts from an early age. To watch a child of 1–2 years and notice the incredible range of emotions he or she expresses in a given half hour is extraordinary. Through testing our limits of spontaneity; in being angry when someone really invades our integrity, and by crying when we hurt, we can later learn how to care about the real needs of others and begin to know a little of what loving is about. Therapy helps us to find what early in life we have lost.

Feelings happen with or without our permission, even if we can pretend not to feel. Most of us are full of useless out-dated emotions, unresolved issues from the past and things completely inappropriate to who we are now, and how we are living life. It is impossible therefore to express an emotion in the right way through this maze. It is like looking for a particular garment on the first day of a Harrods' sale, almost impossible. Yet on we drift, unconscious of our choice to change.

Why should feelings be good or bad? It is only that we label them so – they are simply energy which, if not bottled up, can have good clean use. Fear protects, and anger defends our boundaries. Sadness releases and opens the heart. Compassion unites us and joy uplifts. Fear is closest to the surface, anger and sadness seem intermingled going deeper. Joy and compassion come from somewhere in our interior self, and unfold as we clear away the others. Each has its own level, and can only be released on that level. When feelings have become too much to express we slide upwards out of the body and live life from the head – cut off from experience, avoiding our own 'untidiness'. Rather like not moving the sofa when hoovering, we 'pretend' that what is apparently hidden on the surface is not there.

Mind/body therapies of all kinds have made a huge contribution to our getting in touch with what is really inside us and letting go of what we think might be. This involves being honest with ourselves.

Can we surrender to our human-ness, living the pain and despair, the separation, the longing for wholeness that takes us from relationship to relationship in our search for ourselves through another? At some point hopefully we remember how it was before the separation – and soon we will remember there is no need to forget! Being at one with all the knowing is being at one with the divine lover.

Many of our diseases carry memories of no sense of 'self', only the denial of life. In radiation disease there is no protection of the membrane of the cells. If we radiate outwards, nothing can touch us. The ability to use the divine energy to interact with nature to prevent disaster and create balance is freely there for us all, yet we mostly close ourselves off from this source.

I feel that we age because we become tired of life, tired of the load we carry. We 'wear out' when there is no need to! In our clearing of the emotions, we re-live many deaths, and so go through the fear of it. The violence we have experienced in lifetimes makes our fear colossal. Clear it out! Do not avoid the opportunity to be with the dying, to journey with them a little, to watch their surrender to what is beyond and watch the light in their eyes in that moment of knowing that all is life.

I believe we are here to release and move on, not live and pass on to our children. The earth of England is saturated with thought forms from aeons of time – heavy and trapped in a 'mist' – even the tone of the language is heavy and full of woe. Those born in that country have chosen, as do the peoples of all other countries, to be part of its resurrection and have a responsibility to reach to the sky and bring heaven down – and live it by radiating it on earth. Fear creates only death and denial.

How easy it is to become dependent on the dependence of

those that depend upon us (for more on co-dependency, see Chapter 12)! Here again is the need for scrupulous honesty with ourselves. Although today our complexities are being further unravelled and further understood by psychology, creating a revolution in human capacities, it still requires great courage and commitment to face and own parts of ourselves, and it is so easy to get stuck, or talk ourselves into complacency.

Losing sight of motivation can so easily leave us stuck at base camp, reading and thinking about taking the next step, but not actually doing anything about it. This is like darting around the swimming pool, looking at the water from different points, putting off the moment of jumping into the water to experience it. My going to the USA and studying Ilana's work so that I could work with others, was in fact studying myself so that in knowing where I was with myself, I could also know where someone else might be.

Disease became lack-of-ease on different levels as I began to travel layer by layer down into myself. To begin with I was fearful of the judgements of others, and ashamed, wanting to hide what I found before I realized that the ingredients handed out at conception are, by and large, much the same for us all. Back and back I travelled with endless discoveries of the pieces of my jigsaw surfacing, until I could see that a part of our being is subject to death and rebirth, yet the all-knowing part knows no death, only the separation at conception of what was whole.

In mystical law, Paul Solomon taught us that conception and birth are described as deaths, being the separation from the whole as I have earlier mentioned. This began to explain why the further back I went, the more it felt like dying. Yet on coming back each time the sense of love and compassion was stronger. Was this what Paul called the soul remembering the 'divine lover', that we each leave to make our journey through our human-ness? And in our longing for this inner union, forgotten and unconscious since birth, we search the earth for the partner that can fill this loneliness: until we reach the realization that that aspect is not in another, but is the part of ourself, the Light-spirit, that we left behind.

When we awaken this 'sleeping beauty' part of us we invite

again the forgotten union of the heart, and then we move beyond therapy and techniques, and begin another cycle; our energy becomes lighter and more laser-like, and the work becomes simpler, and less becomes more once again.

PATTERNS OF DISEASE TRAPPED IN THE BODY

I was now starting to evaluate the role my feelings were playing in causing me physical problems – in effect the close links between my state of mind and the state of my body which was by now causing too much pain to continue to deny it.

Feelings are real, they are the outward expression of energy from body and mind in any one moment. All unexpressed feelings can become toxic and, when repressed, can come to the surface as lumps, skin disorders, clots, tumours, spasms, migraine headaches and many other conditions. I decided the only real healthy option was to befriend my locked-up emotions and find a way of expressing them.

Fear, anger, sadness – my route to joy, freedom and compassion has been through these three. Without the experience of fear, anger and sadness, we simply separate from them and 'ice' over the top by being 'awfully nice' and very sentimental. I was taught well!

We are all scared, and angry and sad. By walking through our own experience of these we learn about compassion – first for ourselves and then with others. It is a big step to acknowledge and accept these three emotions as ours, since society teaches us to deny them, and praise is given for control of them. To have cancer or rheumatoid arthritis brings acceptance and attention from others. 'Rise above' we are told, but when a real life challenge arises we find we have not risen above, and all wells to the surface. If you think you can or have transcended these emotions, put yourself in the kind of situation that might involve these emotions and test them!

Perhaps what is needed is for us to be able to express our feelings honestly in the present moment and thus purify our anger – that it is 'clean'. In our sharing of pain we share our human vulnerability.

If we cleanse the air, water, fire and earth in ourselves, we cleanse the planet too – it is that simple.

The body, as I have said before, holds the memory of every experience we have ever had back through time to the beginning. I found patterns of dis-ease trapped within my body including those of my grandparents on both sides of my family. It has taken me 35 years, (not full-time!) to release these, but I feel I have now cleared out of my system the patterns of my ancestors! During this lengthy process my mind has been the observer while what came to the surface were the sort of memories that confuse us, and can make us fear we are crazy. We are not crazy, but rather suffering the complications of delayed grief and outrage of many generations in our families. I watched the different happenings pass through my conscious mind as though I were watching a movie clip, seeing now so clearly that what I might have thought to be the problem was not in fact so.

Our childhood is stored up in our bodies, which are not just bodies which have inherited traits from our parents, but they are the bodies of our parents and grandparents which continue to live on in our bodies, right back to the beginning of time and even include our inheritance of the animal and mineral kingdom within us. The whole past continues to live in us until it is transformed in energy. I suspect this is so. I must have surprised a few dormant genes in my makeup!

We also have angelic inheritance – its sounds, its vibrant colours, and the sense of bonding in joy of our love of the heart. This is almost indescribable in words, yet it is possible to experience, once the denser levels of emotions and worn-out beliefs have melted. We are all of this, here and now, and sadly we have forgotten it beneath the fear and pain which cover our anger and guilt and, deeper still, our shame and self abuse. Daring to journey further we can re-discover this that is forgotten and buried.

Here then, briefly, is how I have found the different areas of the body hold memories trapped in beliefs and feelings.

Head

Difficulty with authority, my own or other people's. To refer
to people as 'big heads' is a way we describe intellectuals and
those motivated by this area of the body.

Headaches

Often as a result of separating from bodily experiences. The
head represents our ideas, or being controlled by them. Heads
get separated from the body experience by fear, closed throats
and tight upper chests. All the energy centres of the body are
represented on the head. Guru equals 'godhead', equals someone to look up to, which in turn equals reflecting attitudes to
authority.

Ears

Something I do not want to hear; this goes for things unspoken
too. Things that are too painful to hear, can result in deafness.
There is a great need for us to listen deeply both to ourselves
and to each other. My third daughter's deafness altered as I
worked firstly on her legs and then on her stomach.

Nose

Our life-force which is breath is connected to the sexual
organs. The blocking of sinuses is the blocking of consciousness; on another level it is the congestion of emotions in the
head.

Eyes

Our capacity to see, in our lives and around us, and into
ourselves. Those with far sight often do not see what is in front
of their noses – like eagles, as the American Indians say.

Short-sighted people on the other hand, like mice, only see
what is immediately around them and have difficulty with the
larger picture of life. Bad eyes inherited from parents are
simply a stronger pattern of not seeing, sometimes to the point
of blindness. There are many levels on which we see or can be
blind to. Spectacles help to diffuse the sight so that if, for
example, an experience has to be endured in childhood there is
a sense of protection and separation: if I do not have to see it,
it is not there. It would seem we all need to use protection in
our early lives, in one way or another, often at the level of
survival.

It is interesting to note the subtle changes in the body particularly at the back of the neck, when spectacles are removed.

Mouth

Directly connects to the stomach, to the arch of the foot, and
to our feelings. The lines around the mouth depict trapped
emotion, as in a clenched jaw, which demonstrates holding
on to life or anger. Lockjaw can reveal severe, frozen,
unexpressed anger.

Neck

The 'hips' of the head are the gateway or birth canal from our
'ideas and ideals' to our 'experience' in the body. We express
ourselves through the throat – how we 'sound' in the world.
Cancer of the throat relates to holding on to what we would
like to say and instead saying something else; a fear of being
put down or not being heard. Our identity is affected and a
lump of deep anger forms. We can draw our necks into our
chests in shame and fear of being seen.

Shoulders

Here sits the load we carry in life, whether real or imaginary. If
I think I carry a load, then that is real for me. The left shoulder

protects the heart and the right carries responsibility for the worldly self – in my self-image in a hunch. Frozen shoulders come from feelings that I dare not experience; life that I dare not live.

Arms and Hands

These move our heart out into the world. It is interesting in family drawings how often hands are omitted. Withered or shrunken arms suggest drawing away from expressing life; lifeless arms mirror a lifeless heart. The right hand goes outwards towards life as the sword of truth cutting a way. In ceremonies, Our Queen holds the sword of truth in her right hand as she carries in her left hand the orb representing the past. Our arms have also to do with trusting others emotionally.

Fingers

Index finger relates to ego and fear, the middle finger to sex and anger, the ring finger to unions and grief, and the little finger to family and pretence.

Chest

In this area we carry our fear-orientated diseases and our commitment to life on earth.

Lungs

These are our connection to life. Our breath brings us into the body to connect with our human-ness or takes us out further into the mystical universe. It is closely inter-connected to the heart, the nose and the mouth, and the lower stomach where we carry our gut feelings. Different feelings result in our changing the rhythm of our breath. Shock, if severe enough, can stop it altogether, freezing us in a moment in time until at a later date another shock sets us off, reawakening the earlier one! The frozen memory of fear may be lodged in the chest where we bury it until we are ready to find it again, although we remember the fear unconsciously each time that memory is touched in everyday life.

Heart

This is the human feeling centre. The releasing of pain and despair opens the heart; heart attacks occur when life is cut off from the heart through great fear. When we deny ourselves joy and love the heart on some level shrivels and, metaphorically speaking, becomes cold; the blood then has more difficulty in circulating and getting back there, which results in disease. The lower legs are affected and can become ulcerated and gangrenous. The heart also relates to the genitals.

Breasts

Pain and disease in this area relate to the gentle feminine nurturing that we did or did not have and to the mothering of ourselves. It is easy to deny giving to ourselves one or all of these qualities if we have not known them in childhood.

Back

The back and spine are critical to our ability to hold ourselves up and the will to go on. A crumbling spine is symptomatic of giving up; to dislocate the spine shows an inability to stand up alone; a sense of life being too heavy, discs that have fused together and collapsed into each other are more about muscles and fluids than the structure and so connect to our feelings and mental beliefs. The upper back relates to the godself and the lower back to the human self and physical peril. The pelvis through which we are born is also the choosing point of life or death as we descend into matter – our trusting to life here on earth. Attitudes get crystallized in the spine.

Internal Organs

Liver   This is usually the first organ to collapse under emotional strain and is associated with anger; it can affect the right shoulder and the eyes and result in headaches.

Pancreas   Represents digestion on all levels; ie. the physical level; the digestion of our emotions and the digestion of life and its experiences – for example not being in the body enough, and therefore having all sorts of unearthly experiences that we cannot assimilate and integrate into everyday life. It has to do with shock in early days and pre-birth trauma such as I describe with my second daughter. In drinking coffee we stimulate the mind and thereby the pre-birth trauma and inhibited action. But also coffee helps us to act.

Kidneys   When diseased these show an inability to let go emotionally. They are strongly connected to deep grief, frozen fear, and lack of trust in life.

Bladder   This is related to the kidneys, but is mostly to do with fear.

Genitals   These represent our identity on a physical level and relate to gender and all that surrounds our birth.

Legs

Legs hold our feelings and beliefs about support physically, emotionally, financially, or any other way. Thighs and calves hold feelings from the stomach, often about not wanting or daring to go forward into life. With a sense of no support in the legs the shoulders rise up. In one case the frozen fear of emotional mistrust manifested as polio in the left thigh, in loosening this memory, it directly connected to the right shoulder and arm, which became too heavy to lift up.

When my mother had her stroke in her right side, I found my right arm too heavy and painful to lift.

The Right Leg steps out into the world, representing the sense of identity, and will usually relate to the father's patterns, our physical strength, and the masculine aspect of ourselves in connection with support and being supported.

The Left Leg I call the leg of the past, since it holds memories of what we have received in life and our relationship to trusting our own more feminine aspects and to being open to receiving from others in connection with heart feelings and the nervous system. It holds memories connected with our emotional relationship to ourselves and our mother. Manipulating mothers contribute to a sense of no emotional support and an inability to receive it in their sons and daughters. To break the lower left leg therefore connects to the lungs, heart and nervous system.

The Knees contain patterns of adolescence and puberty, the fear of growing up and standing alone as an adult. Knees can freeze rather than cope, for fear of failing to do so, and are connected to kidneys and trust. The inability to bend the knee can be an attitude of self-righteousness and inflexibility, of refusing to bend.

Ankles a further feeling of no support being, as it were, frozen to the spot by the crystallizing of the ankles, as in arthritis or a break. What is found in the ankles will also relate to the hips and lower back and to the wrists and base of the skull, since all of these are 'hip' areas.

Feet

These carry all that we are out into life. They hold memories of our very earliest years, including gestation and our contact to the earth. When flat there is a heaviness and a sense of a collapse of life. When the arches are high the stomach and its feelings are withdrawn from the earth. Toes, when either curled back or squashed, show resistance to going forward. They relate to our heads. The very top of the big toe, like the top of the thumb and the pineal in the head, connect to preconception. A bunion on the left foot relates to the feminine aspect, being turned in and therefore a resistance to going straight. The right bunion reads the same for the masculine aspect of ourselves. This information is taught and practised in the Metamorphic Technique.

Accidents

These are our expression of pent-up anger and frustration at not being able to have something our own way, and are therefore to do with authority. I agree with Louise Hay that when we are angry at ourselves, when we feel guilty and feel a need to punish ourselves, an accident is a good way of doing it. It seems as if it is not our fault, we are but helpless victims of fate. An accident allows us to turn to others to receive attention and sympathy, and to let them take responsibility for us. We can even get a time to rest in bed and think. For some of us this is the only way that we are able to take time to listen to ourselves. Instead of getting 'flu' we get 'pain'.

Where this pain occurs in the body gives us a clue as to which area of our lives we feel guilty about or are stuck in. The degree of physical damage lets us know how severely we felt we needed to be hit and where, and also how long the sentence should be, which all adds up to having a very low esteem somewhere inside. The pattern of how the various areas of the body interconnect can easily be learnt and the blueprint of ourselves may be followed just as easily. My own dis-ease was on many levels simultaneously and I find this in many of the cases with which I work.

The Metamorphic Technique puts dis-ease in this way: where it relates to the fluids in the body the dis-ease is within the emotions, feelings or spiritual aspect of the person. Dis-ease in the bones and joints is within the structure of that person, forming our foundations. If here, it is likely to be on the other levels as well. The oak beams are crumbling! Disease elsewhere is tied up with our mental attitudes and beliefs, our resistance to go forward and risk living.

Here is an example. Blisters and ulcers involve both skin and fluids and therefore relate to mental resistance and emotional stress. If these are on the lower left leg, as earlier referred to, there will be a poor connection to being here on earth, because of no emotional support or trust also affecting lungs and heart.

With mental illness it is as if we are possessed by the mind and its illusions, which disconnect us from the reality of experience.

Our healthy dependency as a baby and child results in our becoming interdependent as our emotional maturity grows and we heal the hurt child. We then play out with our lovers our need to depend until that need can mature into interdependency and we can stand alone. The trees grow side by side and are dependent only on themselves, both for their roots to grow down into the earth and for their branches to reach upwards to the heavens, so it is with man in that we are born alone and die alone.

ELEVEN

ANGER, DENIAL
AND ADDICTION

To everything there is a season, and a time
To every purpose under the heaven.
(ECCLESIASTES, 3,i)

Anger protects the violation of our personal boundaries. Clean anger is sharp, quick and needs no explanation. 'Unclean' anger – when anger is not expressed openly and directly but obliquely, and it therefore becomes loaded up with all the past's unexpressed anger – can literally feel like being possessed, being completely out of balance. Yet this is how anger is most commonly registered and that is because it is the most disallowed, non-acceptable emotion in our society! 'Nice people are not angry.' In the body we can see locked jaws, blazing eyes, clenched fists, jutting chins, raised voices, stiffened backs. This distinctiveness of imploded anger we see everywhere today. When anger is used authentically it can often shock us into a sympathetic understanding of why the person did what he did as, for example, in invading your boundaries and coming too close.

Anger, judgement, guilt. Most of us carry these in huge proportions. They are the most damaging and self-destructive emotions and lead to such dis-eases as arthritis, ME, cancer and anorexia, to name but a few.

Anger when suppressed has 'sidelines' such as cynicism, sarcasm, forgetfulness and other passive-aggressive behaviours. We see these more easily in other people. These normal human emotions become so minimized that feelings are hardly experienced at all, so there is no pain, shame, anger or fear; but also no joy or pleasure. These people exist in a state of numbness. If doors are unlocked at all it is usually their children who unconsciously do it.

By being so closed down these people collect partners and family who play out their feelings for them – denial creates its polarity. Self-hate and self-destruction will in its time manifest in the physical body as dis-ease. In betraying others they eventually betray themselves.

There is now much documented evidence to support the fact that the stress of living with pent-up or explosive feelings contributes to disorders such as high blood pressure, heart disease, arthritis, cancer, migraine, ME and a number of others.

What we achieve in this world seems to be subtly tied up with how much we care for ourselves and our fellow man. So, as many of us carry the seeds of self-destruction within us, is outwardly accomplishing something great in life a way of transforming that self-destructiveness without having to go through the emotions? Do we thereby create the situation where others play out our unwanted, unowned emotions for us? In so doing, do we not create abusive behaviour as well as destruction?

To fail is not to take on the challenge of life, but to die does not mean we have failed.

In living life fully, the body can lighten and change but if someone then chooses death, on top of denying the challenge of life, it is likely to create anger in all those around him or her.

If we are uncomfortable with experiences in our lives, we tend to suppress them and then forget them. We suppress them to deny their existence; erasing them – we assume – by deliberately trying to forget them. We do this with our anger. Our unconscious also holds memories of repressed genetic patterns from many generations, as I discovered in my journey to the edge of life and by allowing myself to experience the different feelings that had led in each different case in my family to manifest in a different dis-ease.

We return then to life here to experience again all the possibilities of being human. The more we inwardly deny, the more we outwardly attract in daily life that which will help stir

what is unconscious back again into the conscious mind. I
believe that it is possible to heal everything if we truly live
in the present – in our be-ingness. In our shame and self-
judgement, in our inability to open ourselves to each other, to
give and receive or love, we close the door of our hearts.
Society promotes this dysfunction.

Life then, is lived in a dysfunctional way, with people harbouring a deep fear of society and the world and not deserving
intimacy.

Our rebels in society are outraged for not being accepted,
when in reality it was the picture the parents painted of being
'pillars of society' that lies under their angry feelings. Parents
like these cause children to feel they are failures, because they
have so little time for them. The child's belief is that if I have
more value, my parents would pay more attention to me.

To live with this belief gives a very heavy sense of having
failed. I believe that my own father carried such a major
degree of unconscious suppressed anger towards women, that
at birth I experienced this as 'I would rather you were "dead"
than a girl'; this carried enormous guilt for me; and such outrage that I, in feeling that every day my life was threatened
because he wished I was 'dead' unconsciously, and in self-
defence I wished him 'dead'.

And this was my dear and gentle father whom outwardly I
adored!

I have acted this pattern out in my relationships by deeply,
unconsciously, wanting my partner 'dead' (within my control
so that I could feel safe). To protect themselves, both my
husbands became angry enough with me to want me 'dead' .
This was the depth of the threat we were to each other.

This is a pattern which calls for major survival; and for
myself when confronting it, I became aware of a definite shift
at that causal level of my being.

I suspect this is how curses in families come to be so strong
and difficult to break.

Society's attitude to feelings is hardly a healthy one either. It
demands control – at all costs. Remain 'dignified' and if in any
doubt at all then suppress your feelings to the minimum; and
be sure to dominate others into not feeling either, using power
through words, institutions, or codes, that are only now

starting to be questioned. Girls may swallow their anger and smile and be nice. Boys are to remain unmoved and numb.

Even metaphysics does not encourage the acceptance of anger. We do not yet know how to handle it, and so society is full of 'nice' people in a state of tension and depression, harbouring feelings of wanting to punish everyone and everything. Anger destroys our integrity, spontaneity, and self esteem, and affects our trust in others. We dare not be angry for fear of rejection so we stifle it in control.

Sexual relationships are one of the tools we use to establish power and dominance over others, instead of allowing them to be a means to empower us, and to engender communication and bonding. The effect of angry sex is that the energy remains trapped in the loins, intense but trapped. Sex experienced this way (as I say in Chapter 13) cannot include the heart and the mind, and because of this, the person is therefore never satisfied. In its way it is a form of self-punishment, through withholding the deeper level of communication with the partner.

We can use guilt in a way that makes others depend on us; and so deprive them of the ability to stand on their own feet. We do this mostly with our children and within families.

Where there is a need for dependence, wean gently the one who loves you so well. In allowing another to do harm to us, we in fact harm the other person. We can feel guilty for allowing ourselves to be abused and carry the resentment and anger for years. We can help each other so much to cut the ties by resolving it through communicating clearly. So often what we imagined to be the facts were not so for the other person.

Our inability to acknowledge anger can also manifest in guilt, or we can turn it into self-pity as we become the victim of our pride.

Anger includes within it our need to keep others within our belief system. It includes our fear of feelings. To be 'nice' is such a good disguise for being utterly outraged. It is simply not human to be always 'nice'. Angry people stay busy, are often 'do-gooders' in society, as they move around with tight jaws, speaking through clenched teeth. Then there are those who use intellectual detachment to avoid their feelings of anger. And there are those who cover up an anger which has existed since childhood by mythologizing their past, dressing it up as having been perfect and thus separating themselves from its reality.

In issues of power we create the very thing we deny ourselves by controlling and dominating, instead of empowering. Repression comes out of a reaction to anger, in feeling something which we do not feel we have the right to feel or express. When the anger surfaces, we disguise it so that it becomes more acceptable; guilt is then experienced, stemming from our not being true to ourselves.

Our society is full of massive passive abuse. Behind every crazy person, dependent on someone or something to keep going, is the one who makes them crazy. Anger and guilt go hand in hand. If we give up our anger and our false image and our struggle, we might have to be who we are, so we keep up the ongoing pretence and denial, and think we are living.

Our law courts penalize the victims instead of teaching responsibility. Guilt can paralyse and make us feel ashamed of ourselves. Guilt is rooted in the judgement of our being. Shame controls our intimacy with others in the belief that we do not deserve it.

To cling to addiction helps us to stay distracted from our being. It is something safe and reassuring. That which I cannot do without becomes a substitute for what I dare not risk, in case of failure.

To get beyond co-dependency (for more on this, see pp. 100 ff) we go back to the patterns in the parents and grandparents through whom we came. When young we do not have the frame of reference of experience. Adults have to make sense of things. When someone – especially someone we love – behaves inappropriately and treats us badly, we do not see the behaviour as connected to that person's problem or addiction. We do not understand that it is their issue not ours. So, with no reference, we conclude it must be our fault and that there is something wrong with us. Because each of us can interpret many different things from the same given message, it is essential that, whatever work of understanding is done with the help of therapy, the two people who have caused the 'awakening' come together to make clear to one another what drove them to act in the way they did. Only then can we cut 'the ties that bind' our hearts in pain and often devastation.

As a child I was surrounded by very fearful and controlling people and so, as an adult, these were the qualities in close relationships that I attracted until I became fully conscious of them through M.A. (the Judge) and could take control of my own emotional life which had been so severely damaged.

To resolve the relationships with those in our families, Louise Hay has the following suggestion. See yourself as a child of five or six. Now allow this child to become very small, small enough to fit into your heart. Put it there so that whenever you look down, you can do so with love, as you see the little face looking up at you. Now visualize your mother as a little girl. Reach out and hold her in your arms and tell her you love her; tuck her into your heart beside your own child. Then take an image of your father. See him as a small boy. Feel his feelings. Let him also become very small, so that he too can fit into your heart. Now the three little children can love one another and you can love them all.

In doing this exercise you will also find that you can feel through whom a particular family pattern has moved on to another generation.

ALCOHOL AND DIS-EASE

These are the characteristics, given by the National Association of Children of Alcoholics in October 1985, for what we seem to have in common with many dysfunctional families due to growing up in an alcoholic household:

We become isolated and afraid of people and authority figures.

We become approval seekers and lose our own identity in the process.

We are frightened by angry people and any personal criticism.

We either become alcoholics, marry them – or both – or find another compulsive personality such as a workaholic to fulfil our sick need for abandonment.

We live life from the viewpoint of helping and seeking victims, and we are attracted by that weakness in our love and friendship relationships.

We have an overdeveloped sense of responsibility, and it is easier for us to be concerned with others rather than for ourselves.

We get guilt feelings when we stand up for ourselves; instead, we give in to others.

We become addicted to excitement – tension.

We confuse love with pity and tend to 'love' people we can pity and rescue.

We have stuffed back our feelings from our traumatic childhoods and have lost the ability to feel or express our feelings.

We judge ourselves harshly and have a very low sense of self-esteem (sometimes compensated for by trying to appear superior).

We are dependent personalities who are terrified of aban donment. We will do anything to hold on to a relationship in order not to experience the pain of abandonment. We are conditioned to these types of relationships.

Alcoholism is a family disease, usually one is the scapegoat but we all took on the characteristics of that disease even though we did not pick up the drink.

I find if you can reclaim self-worth through the child's re-experience and release of the trapped angry and painful feelings, through therapy, there is not the need to resort to alcohol to suppress them. Vitamins and minerals help greatly in the early stages, to balance the effect the alcoholism has physically had on the system.

TWELVE

DIS-EASE – CO-DEPENDENCY, SHAME AND BETRAYAL

Do not be who you are, because that is not good enough! Do not have fun, it costs money and is not necessary. Do not be open, honest and direct. Manipulate hurt and get others to talk for you; guess what their needs are, and expect them to guess yours! Do not get close to people, it is not safe! Do not disrupt the system by growing and changing! These rules are made not by people but by systems that protect addictions, and secrets, and which keep the craziness in place. People do follow them mindlessly, and pass them on from generation to generation. My family did.

People did not talk in my family, they smiled and withdrew gracefully to 'be useful'. When I tried to step out into life after school and travel and go to art school, and even dared to suggest a career, all were out of the question either financially – which was, I now see clearly, unnecessary – or because I had a lovely home and why was I never in it? Alas, without us children, my mother had nothing to live for. When I married and had mine, she transferred her needs to them and in doing so, relived her early marriage when my father was still alive. However we felt we always 'looked good', and problems and 'bad' feelings were not allowed, because we were 'so lucky'. Once these rules become a part of us, they keep us in line by producing – should we break them – sensations of guilt, shame, and fear, until we can consciously give ourselves permission to look these systems squarely in the face. These same rules were what also conditioned the Judge's mind as mentioned earlier.

I remember a girl with ME I worked with who was utterly

ready to come back into life, but the one thing she feared was giving up the rigid rules she had imposed on herself. So make it all right to change your rules when you are ready to do so – whatever society says! Be direct and honest. It may not feel too comfortable at first: some rules are made as structures to be broken out from.

SHAME

It holds us back from life and keeps us staring at our feet. I found shame hard to label. It lay under many other things such as fear, rage, confusion, guilt, indifference, yet I now know how much of my upbringing was shame-based.

Where there is addiction to anything dysfunctional that one uses to change how one feels, there is shame; be it alcohol, food, drugs, sex, religion or shopping. It comes where there are secrets; perhaps two or three generations of them. Shame adds fuel to the fire of addiction, and is used to protect and keep one's secrets in place.

When the stigma of shame is cast by a look, by words, or the tone of voice used, or later on as adults a voice from the past inside our heads casts the same spell over us, the sensation creeps like an oil-slick right through our bodies, telling us nothing we do or say is enough; and, worse still, that we cannot change it. A sense of heaviness, hopelessness and dread fills our beings.

Shame is a form of control used successfully by parents and society to maintain the status quo. Shame is what we feel in disappointing someone we love. There are of course situations when we act shamefully and know we could have done better; here it is different, but in the most cases it is as victims of abuse, however subtle, or under whatever name, that we learn to experience shame.

Our shame, then, can affect each choice we make, from our partner and job to how we spend our time and who with. Superiority often goes hand in hand with deep shame, in the hopes of not being seen inside. Our shame can prevent us making the choices that bring us fulfilment and contentment because we do not feel good enough. If this is how we feel, then each encounter in life will reinforce this for us, no matter how much good we do, or how successful we are outwardly. It can even cause us to destroy what is good, and what we really want to attain. Shame leaves us believing that even apologizing for existing at all falls short of what is needed. Although what we do may be OK, what we are simply is not.

Shame comes in attacks, sometimes mild and sometimes severe. Some people live in constant shame. I suspect my mother did. However it comes, trace it as with other feelings back to its roots. There is much shame connected with rules around intimacy and sexual issues in Western society; another is the shame of putting myself before my children or family. To be good with others we must take care of ourselves too. Take a look at the trees of nature that grow side by side, dependent only on themselves for the growth of their roots into the earth, and the reaching up of their branches to heaven. So it is with man.

CO-DEPENDENCY

Here is a list used by Lynn Buess and others in their work with co-dependents to define what is fast becoming recognized as the world's most crippling dis-ease.

My good feelings about who I am stem from being liked by you.

My good feelings about who I am stem from receiving approval from you.

Your struggles affect my serenity. My mental attention focuses on solving your problems or relieving your pain.

My mental attention is focused on pleasing you.

My mental attention is focused on protecting you.

My mental attention is focused on manipulating you 'to do it my way'.

My self-esteem is bolstered by relieving your pain.

My own hobbies and interests are put aside. My time is spent sharing your interests and hobbies.

Your clothing and personal appearance is dictated by my desires as I feel you are a reflection of me.

Your behaviour is dictated by my desires as I feel you are a reflection of me.

I am not aware of how I feel; I am aware of how you feel. I am not aware of what I want; *I ask you what I want.* If I am not aware, I assume.

The dreams I have for my future are linked to you.

My fear of rejection determines what I say or do.

My fear of your anger determines what I say or do.

I use giving as a way of feeling safe in our relationship.

My social circle diminishes as I involve myself with you.

I put my values aside in order to connect with you.

I value your opinion and way of doing things more than my own.

The quality of my life is in relation to the quality of yours.

How many of these statements apply to you? Is it not time we moved from such dependency? For many, I now know, it is life-threatening for them to do so, and thus have to depend on themselves.

CO-DEPENDENCY AND BETRAYAL

Lynn Buess in her book *Children of Light, Children of Denial* illustrates healthy and unhealthy overlapping within family relationships, as shown in Figure 1 (overleaf).

If in a family the mother had no intimacy with her husband she will turn to her male child and 'depend' on him for her needs, so that the child grows up having very little sense of who he is, other than in the context of 'making others happy'. As an adult he will unconsciously then look for a partner like his mother to relate to, yet at the same time not notice his enormous anger as he continues the pattern of making others

Healthy interdependent couple

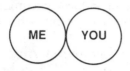

Here we touch together yet are apart, and so strengthen, support and balance each other. This then is a healthy relationship.

Unhealthy dependent couple

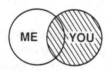

I depend on you. If you cannot be happy I can help you; even in losing myself. This is called today a co-dependent relationship.

Healthy Family

Here the child has a piece of both parents but mostly of itself. Out of this dependency the child learns ways to survive alone, and move into inter-dependency with the parents.

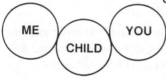

Figure 1

'happy' and negating himself. No one is there for him to depend on, just as it was in his childhood. To add to this he is also dependent, so he also fears leaving such a relationship.

Husbands become dependent on daughters in just the same way. In cases where we act the opposite by rebelling against the parents' dependency, we are not free as we might think, but rather caught in our own anger; reacting out of what our parents are.

Our society does not honour those that stand up and change! It is effectively constructed to concede to dysfunctional behaviour. A child needs love. Most children have not and do not get what they need because mothers are so busy doing what mothers are supposed to do, that they have no time for being mothers. Their children meanwhile will tend to act out what is unconscious within the parents (hence our children are such good teachers) and for this we punish them! If Daddy is a workaholic or he dies, it equals abandonment for the child; and what starts as loneliness and sadness becomes deep hurt; pain that is unresolved becomes frustration, which develops into major repressed anger.

Anger becomes most destructive when not expressed. Angry people feel they must control and have everything their way, even in conversation. They are the ones who are always asking the questions, that way they avoid feeling what's happening inside themselves.

Here are some of the ways we compensate for not being loved: one is by acting the clown who always diverts attention; defusing the arguments and wearing his smile to cover his hurt.

Another is the scapegoat who gets into trouble constantly and causes scandal. Everyone worries about him so they do not have to own what's happening within themselves.

Other disguises we wear are: the martyr, the do-gooder, the religious fanatic, the perpetual traveller, the mother hen, constantly adding to her family.

We all survive through 'games' that we learn from our parents and society. Everyone after all has some qualities that are worthwhile, but it is easier to deny being responsible for them and instead 'pretend'. Our society is full of 'crazy makers' – people who are just 'so nice' and passive and appear to be doing 'nothing' but being polite and amiable. The game they play is that the angrier they feel, the nicer they are to everyone; so no one guesses. They hold on to appalling relationships called 'marriages' (all looks good) rather than re-experience the possible abuse of earlier years, afraid that it will all be too much to cope with. The child of an addictive parent, needs crisis and tension to survive – that's his 'norm'.

Then there is the super-achiever who is driven to look good outwardly, until a crisis breaks his spell.

The loner is a 'nice' compliant, quiet child, feeling that maybe if he keeps quiet, Mum and Dad will get on better. Later, through his own relationships, he wakes up to his denial of self, and his pleasing of Mum and Dad to keep the peace.

Trust has within it the seed of betrayal – betrayal has in it the seed of forgiveness. The struggle to interpret and integrate is what moves us forward to forgiveness.

If the wrong is not remembered by both parties as such, the forgiveness all falls on the betrayed. If this is the case the betrayal is still going on – or has even increased. This dodging of what has really happened is of all the sores the most galling to the betrayed. Forgiveness becomes harder and resentment grows, because the betrayer is not owning his guilt and the act is not honestly conscious. We need, as Jung says, to own and carry our sins and recognize their brutality.

A paradox of betrayal is the fidelity which both betrayer and betrayed keep, after the event, to its bitterness. If we are unable to admit that we have betrayed someone or we try to forget it, we remain stuck in the unconscious brutality of the deed. In this way the wider context of love and fate within the whole event gets missed, and we not only wrong the other, but also ourselves, for we have cut ourselves off from self-forgiveness. We can neither grow in wisdom from the event nor become reconciled, but rather have to wait until such time as we experience the betrayal.

I betrayed my second husband and in my fear refused to look at it until M.A. betrayed me some years later. I then put it right with my ex-husband by admitting my part in his pain, and sharing with him the hurt and resentment of years.

Forgiveness by one requires atonement by the other. Atonement is self-understanding. Conditions now can be transformed within the same close personal situation in which they occurred. This is most effective where there is opportunity for full recognition of the other. This could be called love – unconditional – in that both people go free from the psychic ties I referred to earlier, and are then free to form relationships again.

No matter how horrendous the experience, the trauma, and grief, it does end when we are willing to touch into and move beyond our deepest fears, accepting and releasing our rage, and reclaiming our trapped power. We have to do this part *alone*.

'Love is expecting people to keep their promises,' goes a particular saying. 'Wisdom is knowing that sometimes they do not.'

Self-love is knowing you can handle yourself in the fact that they do not.

Most betrayals are innocent, but it helps the heartbreak so much to have continued communication, however infrequent.

The god within – the Divine Light – the immaculate aspect – is the core of each of us; that place of total and limitless spontaneity, the child in each of us, around which we have built many layers of belief and worn out feelings. Our child is optimistic, creative and hopeful, yet these are the very qualities that cause us guilt instead of Life.

When we have a deep experience, we bypass the protective game-playing layers of ourselves and touch and operate from this finer aspect of our being.

Moving beyond the body and mind into the soul, and resonating with that state, is being 'moved from the depth of one's being'; shattered and overwhelmed by the understanding revealed in that moment.

Our thoughts are the waste product of our thinking; underneath them lies what is dynamic and spontaneous in us. In our emotional lives, deep feelings of the soul tend to get sclerosed into our personal feelings. There are the various levels, from the personal anger and pain through the deeper layers of outrage – as was felt in the Gulf War for what happened to the Kurdish people, in a universal way – and under all this is an immaculate state of being. The Life of Life: Light.

Life's journey takes us in our longing for unconditional love, purity and sacredness, through the hurts and limitations and in this our emotions become tarnished. Be kind to your soul: believe in it and its richness of being – call upon it. Do not adapt to being less than you are; make the environment around you adapt to your richness of being instead of the other way around. If we trust and come from the immaculate within, then others will follow. All of us are drawn as with a magnet to those who express goodness in their lives.

Let us take our beauty with us everywhere. There is no wound that cannot be healed. That is only an idea in our fearful minds. Trust to the regenerative power of life. Let go of the mind's idea that we are all 'handicapped'. I used to think that if I did not show my feelings, if I smiled and was 'nice', and if I kept the conversation light, I was protecting my children and fooling those around me. Now I know that communication works far more poignantly at non-verbal levels, even if we are not always conscious of this. If something does not ring true, we will hesitate to interact.

THIRTEEN

OUR ATTITUDES
TO SEX AND ABUSE

A man is born gentle and soft
At his death he is stiff and hard.
Green plants are tender and full of sap.
Dead, they are dry and withered.
Therefore the stiff and inflexible is the disciple
of death;
The gentle and yielding the disciple of life.
(THE TAO OF I CHING, Chap. 76)

In most strata of society young children are punished for playing with and exploring their bodies, by looks of embarrass-
ment and shame from the adults. These looks often speak
louder than words. I believe that this sort of repression of a
natural instinct lies at the root of our subsequent later sexual
neuroses: memories of the shame and disgrace inflicted by
shamed and disgraced parents and teachers. As I was one of
them, what chance was there for my children not to establish a
connection between sensual self, exploration, shame and punishment? This results in a tendency to spend life repressing
pleasure in order to avoid pain. In this category lie those we
know who remain committed to not 'turning on' any feelings
but remain dull and frigid and closed, so that life itself appears
to have drained away. They are sometimes left with a need to
seek pain in order to find pleasure; the roots of pornography
and perversion can be traced from this source.

If our bodies become our enemies at an early age, albeit

unconsciously, and are to be suppressed, then denial and control become 'good' and to acknowledge and to surrender to feelings becomes 'bad'. Here we get caught between what we feel and what we should do – cut off from our body and controlled by the mind, frozen in no man's land. So what do we do? We begin to *think*! In this moment our sensuality becomes a matter of weighing doubts, fears and other people's needs. We are caught in the four-year-old's memory of punishment, shame and guilt. From my particular experience there was the added bonus in believing sex was only enjoyed by women of lower classes and, furthermore, that men only enjoyed sex with them too.

We cannot let go of a cycle of experience until it is completed. If it is not completed then we seek out our needs directly or indirectly in our outer experiences of life, so that our 'core' may evolve further towards wholeness. The residual energy of unexpressed sexual needs travels with us, and some can even become neurotically fixated by it. The impulse towards self-exploration and stimulation is real. The drive to unfold the answer is very strong. If we cannot express it, we live our emotional life in a state of denial, our arms dead by our sides, pelvis tight, knees locked, jaw clenched, fighting with all our might the 'devil' within.

Alternatively, by following the addictive pattern, we always look for someone outside ourselves to turn us on, so that much of our sexual relating is without feeling or relationship. If on the other hand we are allowed to explore, have fun with our bodies as children, and if our sexuality is accepted and integrated into our self-valuing instincts, then we have a solid base from which to 'play' as teenagers and trust the heart as lovers. For how many of us was our first 'love affair' one of trusting, loving friendship, full of innocence and fun? Sexual energy when it does not flow through the heart feels 'stuck' and the friendship becomes distorted and the lovers' experience is one of lust.

When sex comes from an idea in the mind it is but a fantasy. Sex coming from the desire of the body is a necessity but when sex comes from the heart it is love and our connection will be at the most sacred level. Sex then is essentially meaningless without the heart. For many of us it is this heart connection that we fear most, yet at the same time we long for it. This I believe is due to the latent pain and guilt that we carry trapped in the body. If puberty is denied, it will eventually surface, so it is worth spending time learning how to love both ourselves and others, at this in-between time, lest its energy gets stifled and is misused instead.

In this age of AIDS and early-teenage pregnancies, it is vital that we facilitate ways and outlets, as well as safe sex education, for the expression and development of sensuality throughout our society, and especially for our young people. It is tragic to deny the growth and expression of our hearts because of our shame and guilt. Theatre, arts and dance in their many forms are making great strides to find means that give young people a way to explore and develop their sensual expressiveness and flexibility, to know and trust their body and its feelings through these mediums, so that when intercourse actually happens the experience will be deep and rich, open and trusting, right from the start, instead of doing what is expected.

In our hearts we all know that full sexual relationships should have a genuine loving and trusting friendship. In these circumstances, your lover becomes your teacher of life, and together you explore the unexplorable, ride the heights and walk the depths. It is the heart's connection to another, as mine with M.C. and the Judge, that can endure and help us survive through life's trials, just as the opposite, heartless breaking of that bond, can in turn feel like the breaking of our lifeline. We fear the pain involved for ourselves and thereby cause much unnecessary inward bleeding. It is hard and painful and often life-threatening to stand alone. It certainly has been for me.

Our society is full of suppressed teenagers who go through their puberty in their thirties and forties, ignorance and fear having turned the otherwise exploratory early years into years of restriction. The result is that the energy is still there, and if we do not learn to use it well in love, then we use it in addiction to, for instance, ambition, daring, depression, starvation, drink, drugs, smoking or dare-devil driving/flying. Any of these becomes an addiction when the motivation changes from an experience of life to the enjoyment of sensation.

Sexual malpractice is related to trauma at the post-conceptual period, and in partnerships like will attract like. So although the new partner may in the early stages appear different, within two years the old, unresolved patterns will begin to emerge until in our despair and abandonment, or in our repeated denial, frustration and all-consuming work, we return to complete the unfinished business from within our early sexual stages, learning to love ourselves and give to ourselves in joy with no guilt, re-establishing the vital link again between our loving friendship and sexuality. In doing so, we allow sensuality into friendship, and in our sexuality allow the exploration, trust and open communication that can heal these wounds, fears, doubts, ignorance and repression of the body and the heart, and the cock-eyed beliefs we hold in our minds and which do not work. All of these things only undermine our relationships and marriages, even when they last – and mostly they last because society dictates, or we are too scared of the unknown to take the first step into it and acknowledge the sham.

As we move into the second half of life, our sexuality and love-making incorporate a thousand other forms of caring. How wondrous to arrive at the stage of old age, with the richness and compassion of a friendship of self-mastery through gentleness with oneself and another, and thus be at peace within oneself, with a deep, unafraid heart connection with all other human beings.

Much of this chapter and the last one has focused on the body, the place where we begin and end. As we free the body by unlocking the dis-ease, all kinds of feelings start to flow: old familiar ones, new unexpected ones, good, bad, light and dark. These are all just feelings. Being alive means having a heart and expressing it. In freeing the body we free the heart to express the power of love, the mind to listen and not judge, the spirit to its memory of oneness with light, so that, although in the body, we can express and manifest as the beings of light that we truly are, dependent on ourselves and interdependent with others. What we acknowledge can be healed. What we bury turns to abuse.

ABUSE

Each of us is shaped by his/her childhood. It is here that neuroses are rooted and if not here, then earlier still in gestation. Through therapy we can remember, and re-enact where necessary. Associated happenings in the present act as a catalyst where the process of maturing has been blocked by early trauma, but changes in personality occurring in this time often do not touch the cause.

'To have our helplessness and total dependency taken advantage of by the person we love at a very early age, soon creates an interlinking of love with hate. Because anger towards the loved one cannot be expressed for fear of losing that person, love and hate interlink, and remain an important characteristic of later objective relationships' (Alice Miller). Many people can never imagine that love is possible without suffering and sacrifice and therefore fear being abused, hurt and humiliated. Since abuse must be repressed for the sake of survival, all knowledge that might undo this situation must be fought against by every possible means. This results in a severe impoverishment of the personality and a loss of the vital sense of belonging. Repression cannot eliminate this, but only reinforce it and create the need to compulsively repeat again and again the same trauma either actively, or passively, or both. To abuse one's children for ones own need either passively or actively, although the former carries the deepest trauma, is one of the ways we perpetuate this trauma – and is far more alarming in that overall it goes unnoticed – we call it 'upbringing'.

It is difficult for those of us that were the 'property' of our parents to realize that we are treating our own children in the same way, as our property, unless we are finding out about ourselves. In many cases where parents have themselves been isolated and emotionally deprived, their child is the only permissible and safe object for the sharing of their affections. It seems that the greater our refusal to face the past, the more incomprehensible its neurotic and psychotic manifestations are in the next generation. It is an illusion to think that bygones are bygones . . . any one exploring even the edge of their subconscious knows that.

'An unacknowledged trauma is like a wound that never heals over and may start to bleed at any time' says Alice Miller. 'In a supportive environment it may become visible and finally heal completely. To conceal the most dramatic aspects of our lives under a banner of silence and denial, is the overture to an early death. Through denial, whether of facts or feelings, we become alienated from ourselves, separated from, yet controlled by, the very thing we hide from.' It can be seen that children will sometimes pay for their parents' silence with pathological symptoms. Through grief we arrive at reconciliation, whereas guilt freezes and cements and numbs into dis-ease.

In journeying through our own childhood traumas, we are in a far better position to help others through theirs.

The specific ways by which parents unconsciously communicated their war experiences to their children through their silence, and inability to look again at the pain and horror of their experiences, lived on in their children as it did in me. It is hard indeed for these children to re-make the connection with those intense feelings. Alice Miller speaks most interestingly about her work with children of parents of the Third Reich. For myself I remember my work in Germany in the 1980s drawing to the surface in me the sound of war, as if I could see the soldiers marching over the fields, and was caught in the aggression and control of those drilled men, hiding their own fears as they headed for the unknown – war. One morning, after dreaming war and fear, a young German doctor, tall, blond, and gentle, who was a superb interpreter for my work, suddenly became my young, blond tall father saying goodbye, when we and he all unconsciously knew he would not return. I could hardly believe the intensity of my feelings of helplessness and despair, and later rage, as the trauma of the four-year-old left alone with my questions and pain at the time of his departure for war came to the surface.

There are many people who have gone hungry all their lives even though their mothers were conscientious, and saw that they got enough food and sleep, and cared for their general health. That these people could nevertheless be deprived of what was most crucial to them seems not yet to be understood, even among professionals. It has not yet become common knowledge in our society that our child's psychological nourishment comes from the understanding and respect provided by those to whom he first becomes attached, and that child rearing and manipulation cannot take the place of this nourishment, neither can food.

We cannot undo the harm and abuse done to our children but perhaps we can help prevent future damage by uncovering some of the causes, and not needing to defend ourselves or our parents. Unless society faces what is happening the more frequently the traumatization will occur. The fact that children are sacrificed to their parents' needs is an uncomfortable truth that none of us likes to hear. Parents are, after all, also victims of their own childhoods.

Alice Miller says 'the source of creativity lies in the person's capacity for suffering, not in his neurosis. Freedom and the ability to love come by experiencing traumatic childhood situations and articulating the resulting hatred and despair, not by acting them out in life.'

Change in society comes about by uncovering and recognizing the truth in its entirety not by manipulative methods based on the acceptance of social taboos.

To achieve genuine insight is a slow process in which intellectual knowledge plays but a small part, alas. To rely on it will bring both sorrow and conflict of loyalties, but we can succeed in gaining the freedom that I now know exists for us on the other side of sorrow. We can look back and decide for ourselves our journey's value and in this then we have the possibility to use our eyes, our ears and our intuition to take what we perceive seriously. A.M. refers to the Fourth Commandment and the traditional methods of child-rearing, which go to make up our denial of childhood trauma. I have written of my personal journey, which may be similar, but can never be exactly as another's, yet how we integrate new insights into our existing fund of knowledge will depend largely on the character of the person. My writing this book is not to win support for my discoveries, but rather to hope that it may challenge others to make their own discoveries to freedom from dis-ease.

It has taken the 1980s to bring child abuse to the public's notice. In England it was triggered largely by the Government's enquiry at Cleveland. Knowing some of those involved, I listened to the evidence. We are observing a new situation – not that sexual abuse of children is new, rather to the the contrary – but it is new for the facts to be discussed in public; and this gives hope that the victims will now have a chance to work through their confusion, isolation and disturbed perception of reality instead of unconsciously passing it on.

What behavioural patterns does a person sexually abused in childhood bring to society? We have not been able to ask this before, as the information has just not been available. Furthermore, many of those in the psychoanalytical field deny the cruelty inflicted on children by infantile sexual abuse.

The question of what children do with their unresolved trauma, of how later – as adults – they turn the cruelty to which they were subjected against themselves and others, has never really arisen in psychology. Alice Miller asks in her book, *Thou shall not be aware*, 'What is the significance of the fact that 80% of all female drug addicts and 70% of all prostitutes were abused as children?.' I know there to be many levels of subtle abuse.

In working with such trauma the unconscious message of people severely wounded in childhood is that they deny the wounds and idealize their parents and childhood while, at the same time, blame themselves for all the suffering. They keep secret from themselves and others that which also allows them to escape the confusion, until they can face the truth. I believe the extent of sexual abuse of children runs throughout all levels of society to a far greater extent than is generally thought and it is now coming to light how the blocked feelings resulting from such abuse inevitably lead to deep disturbances. If we look back in time we can see that it has been customary, and permissible, to misuse children to fill a wide variety of adults' needs. They provide cheap labour, they are an outlet for our pent-up feelings, our sense of inferiority, an opportunity to exercise power or obtain pleasure. Through them we project our conflicts and fears. Last of all, sexual abuse, due largely to how we handle sex in our society, holds a deep sense of shame.

We hit and humiliate children in the name of discipline and

demean and torment them in the name of 'having fun'. This is acceptable and happens quite openly. Sexual abuse, on the other hand, usually takes place in a hidden way, and often in darkness. We cannot achieve integration alone, for the shame, fear, pain and betrayal that is experienced, the guilt, isolation and helplessness, leads our hate of action merely to bury and repress the experience. Added to this is the adult's bewildering silence and the contradiction between his deeds and the principles he upholds in daylight. All this leads to intolerable confusion for the child. If as children we are talked out of what we perceive, the unconscious re-enactment in later life will be lazy and defused in the memory of what happened originally; and we will question if it all is not really just fantasy.

Take for example a two-year-old sexually abused by the nanny, and thereafter by her brother, growing up and struggling to avoid abuse, but finding that she repeatedly attracts situations in which this happens. Unconsciously we do this with any trauma, until we remember, and can begin to articulate and talk about it. Without a supportive person to listen to us, we repress it again and again, and even devise theories to ward off further experience – one of which is to choose a therapist skilled in talking us out of, instead of into, the experience, with the result that the victim of abuse continues to feel responsible for what has happened to them.

More than 80 years ago Freud claimed he had established that his patients' memories of being sexually abused as children by adults were not memories of real events, but only fantasies. How many countless times have therapists repeated this to their clients? How can we prove such a thing, except with witnesses? In such situations witnesses do not exist for with sexual abuse both parties usually have an interest in keeping it secret, since even by acknowledging the truth the victim then has to own the feelings of shame, guilt and colossal fear. The reality is more tragic perversions and self-destructive enactments. Organizing the present suffering to fit into the denial pattern of the past guarantees that the early unbearable pain remains further repressed.

It is important when unlocking trauma to be provided with a good support system, or else one can find oneself locked in deep depression, or in the chaos of awakened feelings, as I did. Any therapeutic technique is only as good as the person who uses it. Those therapists who have had the opportunity to experience and work through their own traumatic past can truly accompany another on their path to truth and understanding, without confusion, or the need to educate, instruct, misuse, or seduce them because they no longer have to fear the eruption in themselves of feelings that were stifled long ago. From experience comes the healing of these feelings and the joy of finding what has been hidden of oneself.

Gradually those of us that have known abuse and moved on through it are finding our voices, allowing ourselves to listen to the client, beyond any learnt structure – and what we hear fits into *none*.

Child abuse can have lifelong effects, in that society blames the child and upholds the adult's dysfunction, yet the child in us is innocent. A past crime cannot be undone, but by more awareness and further facts much can be done to prevent new crimes of abuse.

A new way of seeing what we are doing as parents is needed instead of denying the victimization of the child. In so doing, I am convinced, the information will reveal what so many of us have had to undergo at the beginnings of life without even knowing about it in later years, and without anyone else knowing about it either. We are on the threshold of future freedom!

As I've said before, and have experienced through my own dis-ease, our childhood truth is stored up in our body and, if repressed, will manifest as dis-ease. Our intellect can deceive us, we can allow our feelings to be manipulated and what we perceive to become confused, and we can trick ourselves with medication. The body presents its disease as the bill for services rendered (and misused). As the child in us remains whole in spirit, accepting neither compromises or excuses, so the body can renew itself continually – and it will not stop tormenting us through dis-ease until we stop evading the truth it is communicating.

Society blames the victim for being weak and dependent and it proclaims those in authority as being above criticism. As a result 'victims' must content themselves with the knowledge that they will not be protected. Instead they will be blamed and humiliated, while those who abuse them will be defended. This attitude on the part of society is reflected in the way abuse is handled by the Courts. In order to protect the culprit from the accusations of their victims our society, including professional experts, stubbornly demeans or glosses over and minimizes the connection between what was endured in childhood and later illness.

Alice Miller writing of Virginia Woolf's trauma of being sexually abused between the ages of 12 to 59 by her half brother, and of her subsequent schizophrenic episodes, ties in with the breathing conditions spoken of and experienced by the abused children in the Cleveland incident and with my own experiences with cases of abuse. Namely, when shock to the system is so great, we retreat up the body, or out of it. Dr Elisabeth Kubler-Ross mentions this in accounting for the butterfly drawings on the walls and in the gas chambers – the children left their bodies before undergoing extermination. It was said in Court that the Cleveland children manifested breathing difficulties in the chest. Shock disassociates us from our body and our feelings. I believe schizophrenia is when the person separates further and, although not dead, is completely removed to a 'mental' state – making no connection to the body, and yet paralysed with a fear of moving in any direction.

The best kept secret, a book by Florence Rush, is a secret no longer. The anonymous cancer in our society has been revealed. Our 'pillars of society' only appear to be 'all together' wearing the right clothing. They are seen in the right places, go to the right schools, just as I did, and have a wife that 'toes the line'. Inwardly our pillars of society are often held together by denial and alcohol. They work long hours to help blot out what really needs attention. Society permits only superficial feelings, anything more is regarded as 'lacking in dignity'.

To stay within this system entails a huge effort of control, not much happiness, and certainly no conversations that might expose one's human vulnerability and 'upset' the rules of the establishment.

Life is mostly a duty – people struggle to get into it, so there is little time for genuine warmth or companionship. Society moves as the bubbles on the sea as the tide goes in and out, separated from its unexpressed feeling as the bubbles on the surface are separated from the deep still waters below on the ocean bed. All is empty inside.

FOR LOVE OF OUR CHILDREN

We often love our children to distraction, but with conditions that he or she perform as the contrived self, rather than giving them what they need. This is no obstacle for an intellectual adult, but it is for a balanced emotional life. It is hard for a person such as this to do other than choke off any true feelings by ridiculing them and attempting to persuade himself they do not exist. The hardest step of all is to break with his fixed attitudes – I call it one foot on the bridge to freedom, but because of early experience it is not possible to cross it. Instead he abandons what he believes leads to danger rather than freedom and repeats his compulsion to hold on to what he thinks is safe. He cements the very thing he is trying so hard to break and thus hates and despises himself, and deeper goes the pattern.

What we drive away from seeing in ourselves, returns to haunt us through our children. Many highly successful people suffer deep depression. The only way to break free is when self-esteem is based on what is automatically felt; and not by possessing qualities of success. So long as it is his qualities that are admired the grandiose person feels unloved for the person he is. Should he fail to achieve the expectations he has set for his survival, he will drive himself ever onwards to achieve more, lest he feel the fear and deep shame that drives him. This is real self abuse; and yet it is not so uncommon.

FOURTEEN

FAR MEMORY
AND MINDFULNESS

Far memory is a curious experience – very real to those that have experienced it and very strange and unreal to those that have no experience to measure it by – like, for example, seeing an angel. If you have had that experience it adds another whole dimension to your life, but if your best friend tells you and you have *no* similar experience by which to measure it, well, you wonder indeed if it might be an idea to change friends.

In my experience going back through the memories of this lifetime – through my birth and back through the gates of pregnancy to my conception and back further to many life experiences that have brought about the patterns that I am living to change now – has helped me to understand many things through re-experiencing them: the strengths and weaknesses I have brought with me, the trapped, 'handicapped' parts of me, and the 'freer' parts where I am at ease. Since the answers lie in our personal histories and it is the body that carries the memories of these histories (as was described in Chapter 10), different areas of the body relate to different patterns, memories and different ages. To go back therefore allows us to get to know our own blueprint in a more tangible way than someone else telling us.

Each life runs in many cycles and each cycle has its lessons with many teachers. A mother can only teach her child what she has herself received. Our mother comes first with our birth and teaches us our relationship to self, she nurtures our first years or she does not. Our father is next in our childhood, as he helps us 'open to the world'. The fact that I lost mine when four years old meant that it was very hard for me to open up and trust the world and those in it. We learn about ourselves in puberty and later in life, as we mature, we expand our learning to our society and planet.

Life is but a mirror through which we see ourselves. So much of the suffering and grief in our personal lives relates to the 'unfinished business' within these early years, which is mirrored in a larger way in society, in our cities, and in the lives of those that run them and sit in office as judges, lawyers, doctors and parliamentarians. For all of us there is a need to bring our personal inner lives in line with our public outer lives, to be whole.

Lynn Buess has been in the consciousness movement longer than I have. Like Soozi Holbeche, he trained with Paul Solomon in those early days in Virginia. Lynn's skills include the Tarot and numerology, which he combines with his extraordinary laser-like ability to pick up the thread of a pattern manifesting today. In all of ten seconds, it would seem, he can see its whole lineage back to the point of Time's existence itself, to the Big Bang and the forming of the Cosmos.

His work has profound effects and he has a delightful humility that goes with what he dares to say. He has written five books and has done considerable work in the field of alcoholism and abuse. When in England he has stayed at my house, which has given me an opportunity to spend many hours in intuitive discussion with this gentle and wise man.

With Lynn's help I was able to go back in time and to see the same patterns repeating themselves over and over again – I could begin to uncover the simple truth of today and my wounds; my chosen challenges for this time around, along with my blessings; the many times before when I had met my children, my parents, my lovers, my friends; and the parts we had played together on another stage at another time, as it then seemed, although I now sense that 'all is now'.

To reclaim the trapped and crumpled parts of ourselves the mind has to be liberated from the past, which then liberates our future as we concentrate on living now. Fears of past pain are no longer there to be projected into the future. We can then give ourselves to life instead of being trapped with 70 per cent of our energy, as Lynn would say, holding back the unfinished business of the past we fear to see, and causing a void or separation between our outer selves and our inner personal lives. We live generally in a very immature culture, hence it is not the 'norm' to be mature, only to pretend to be. Look at the walking wounded in our families and our friends. We no longer empower each other. How can we reach in later life a place of contemplation and wisdom and oneness with the universe? How can we die in peace, knowing our eternalness, if we have not connected to the eternal part of ourselves? How can we do any of this until the 'hurt child' in each of us is healed?

Gabriele Roth, the 'dancing Shaman', whose dance and theatre work has become so popular in Europe in the past five years, suggests we can, metaphorically speaking, direct and star in our own film, or we can play little parts in other's productions. We can choose to be fully aware, or to live life in a state of numbness and blindness. We are students of life and our teachers come and go in many forms. Each step will have its teacher, its lesson to learn and a relationship to be completed. The tying up of knots in order to walk on once again is essential. Few of us manage to do this well, and psychic ties remain, even when people have died, thereby depleting our energies and leaving guilt and frustration as companions, instead of friendship and gratitude for the lessons shared and learnt.

From touching into the experience of times past it is but a short step away to understanding that the body is representing the accumulated listening since the beginning of time. In tapping into these experiences of past lives, I have seen clients' bodies visibly change.

MY EGYPTIAN LIFE MEMORY

The Story

I can see myself in the shimmering white robes and head-dress of an Egyptian priestess of high order in the Temple. My chariot is pulled by lions, and I and others have full command of wild animals and also the elements. All appears bathed in a radiating white light; our communication is mostly through thought. My father is there, and also the young German doctor (whom I referred to earlier). There is absolutely no fear: our life is very spiritual, harmonious and vibrant; there is a great bond of love between us and a sense of reverence for all life.

How This Was Triggered

I was halfway through my three years' training with Ilana Rhubenfeld. During one of the Feldenkrais movements I felt pressure around my forehead and could see a band around it. The next day when I went for my private session Ilana placed her hands on my head and told me to pick up the memory of the headband and to describe the picture I saw. I was at once in Egypt; the colours were gold and white.

My Memory

This is what this particular memory has taught and brought back for me in connection with the qualities I am harmonizing in my life and work today:

1. As a child I would say, when referring to my father, 'He and I are the same colour.' (In Egypt we were both in shimmering white.)
2. The headband had a serpent down the back as worn by those in the Temple at that time.
3. The point between the eyes on the forehead is the point of all-seeing.
4. At the same time as I remembered my ability to 'see', I knew that was not the level which I had chosen in this lifetime to communicate knowledge to earth.
5. My level of choice for now was the heart – the more human level.
6. In that moment the emerald and diamond ring my father gave to my mother on their engagement came into my

awareness: my mother seldom wore it, nor handed it on to my brother on his betrothal as would have been the tradition. The green emerald (green for the heart) surrounded by the 'white' diamonds (the shimmering white of Egypt) became mine on the death of my mother. This I felt, somehow symbolically, was a gift from my father to affirm our dual work.

7. The re-experience of this memory had a profound influence on my life from then on. It somehow gave me permission to re-establish my link to that 'white' level of consciousness – of universal knowledge and understanding – and to know its strength within my being, as in the following years, along with the heart's warmth and gentleness, I watched this opening up in myself. The colour of white – all the vibrations rolled into one – has given me courage, conviction and a patience to allow the 'knowing' to unfold.

My mother always had premonitions: when her twin sister was very ill in India; when my brother's prep school burnt down; when he had meningitis; and before he died – she knew the moment it happened. She also told Nanny when father had died – and Nanny then brought to her the telegram to confirm it.

Before my mother died, my brother and father appeared to say they would be there to help her let go. I was also aware of the very moment she made her decision to let go and die.

Once I took responsibility for what I had come to do, my father's presence began to fade in the following months. I think people choose to do a service like his, staying near Earth until it is completed and they can move on. He and my mother and grandmother all work to 'rehabilitate' people when they go over. I have seen that too.

I have had many 'past-life' experiences: I have had the same parents in other eras; twice before I have killed myself rather than claim my power – and much more. This life has indeed been hard work, and very busy in reclaiming all that was sclerosed in rheumatoid arthritis. All my guidance has been from 'another dimension'. 'We are one another', wherever we are, and as we become lighter, so it gets easier to travel up and down the levels.

I remember an experience many years ago after clearing further 'pockets of the past' with Lynn. He said he would leave the room for five minutes or so as there was more healing to be done, but not by him. It was extraordinary: I could see a band of angels in the most radiant colours who came and lifted my body, as if offering it up to some higher being. I was swathed like a mummy.

The angels sang as they lifted me up and I felt my body become much lighter, and later, when I opened my eyes again, it was as if I had been given a new body altogether. But most of all, I recall the feeling of such incredible love, which had no conditions whatsoever – it was clearly the natural way of being.

Finally, I was aware of a figure behind me, whom I could not see, though just above my head I could see a most beautiful pair of hands – as if in Dürer's painting. They faded and I came back to this earthly dimension. Lynn then came in and asked what had happened.

I have also seen beings from the angelic kingdom appear when working with others – not often, but sometimes. Also, close relations of the client, both dead and alive, will manifest, but it is the feeling and expression of that individual that is important to the client. Sometimes they speak, but at this level it's all in thought. I never interfere, just listen; it's interesting though that both the client and I will hear the same 'thought'.

Now that I am myself completely in the here and now, I notice that these 'unearthly' experiences are much fewer. Everything now seems to be inside me, not outside any longer.

We had a family ghost which my first two children saw and described at the ages of three and four, and on occasions through my life I have been able to see and hear the people of other times in the silence of the hills describe their lives and their battles, their clothes, and so on. This has happened not only in Scotland, but in parts of Turkey and Greece, too.

In my GCE art exam we were given the description of a scene to paint. Years later I found a small oil painting in an antique shop depicting exactly the same scene I had painted in my picture; I still have it.

Now of course many of us are having such experiences of synchronicity. Colossal changes are afoot and we are all being subject to them.

THE PART OF OUR MIND THAT GOES WELL BEYOND FEAR

The depth of the mind is unfathomable – its ability to expand unimaginable, yet we rarely listen long enough or deeply enough to hear anything but what is routine. The calculating, judging part of our mind operates superficially; it needs to control, fitting everything into slots, setting routines. This mind is cramped and cluttered. It fears it might not know everything, and so it pretends that it does. Nothing can then be new, fresh or mysterious. Much of society is trapped there.

There is another dimension of the mind which we can sense, and which many more are now touching. It is independent from our 'know-it-all' analytical mind and I call it the intuitive mind. It is receptive, open, enquiring, alive and listening in the moment. It has all the subtleness, flexibility, range and knowledge from forever. It is there for us all if we know how to listen – how to expand and go beyond the 'know-it-all' judgemental mind. Alas, it gets buried early in our lives by trauma, training, and school. Our teaching educates us out of our natural way of tuning in and listening to our intuition. We begin to doubt and eventually shut off and go the way the teacher says. Usually they themselves have been 'mis-educated'. There is in this respect much corrective work to be done in our schools and through the education system, as our way of learning gets more and more mind-orientated.

Most people have a constant mental gramophone going on, playing the same records of questions, worries, precautions, opinions on what to say, how to act, and who to be, so that our heads are so full of thoughts that there is no room for 'here and now' thoughts to come in from the intuitive mind any more. 'Mindfulness', as taught in Buddhism, involves unthinking and listening – emptying the mind so that there is space for thoughts connected to the immediate moment to enter. This is what I ask my clients to do as we work – to listen under my hands to within their bodies. We think before we speak and before we act. We are always thinking. With our calculating mind running night and day packaging our experiences, we need to return to stillness and silence in our lives, so that we can 'hear' what is really going on in there. We have a choice: we can either allow our minds to run on automatic pilot, so that our lives drift across the surface of reality in a superficial way, or we can deliberately choose to allow the mind and emotions to integrate, thus allowing the mind to be 'part of' instead of 'separated from' our feelings in our living of life. The mind holds the ideas, the body holds the memories of experiences.

Often what we think and what we experience can be so different. Which one then holds the truth? Which is worth following? The intuitive mind links to the experiences from our life while the 'know-it-all' logical mind only separates us from them. For many in our Western culture it is a stiff lesson ever to get behind our separating, protecting, closing-off, analytical mind. No one can choose but ourselves. Life is but a journey of exploration for us all.

The members of our legal profession are trained to think logically and rationally. Their every action is calculated and weighed up. Some also have the ability to go beyond what is logical, to feel into a case, to touch the truth that lies behind it, to be able to ask the questions in a way that can confirm that hunch. That's intuition, not logic. Time and again during my relationship with the Judge I listened and watched this intuitive quality win through the hours of cross-examination in court. Time and time again I heard that same man doubt and then deny what he intuitively felt and wanted in his private life. In allowing will to become willingness, all can change. In will we hold ourselves in check, controlling our lives. But living in willingness means opening to the dawn of something new.

FIFTEEN

MEN AND VIOLENCE

Dr Rosalind Miles, who usually writes on women's rights, has recently published a book on men and violence in society, *Looking for a Kinder Gentleman*, in which she cites a 1988 Department of Justice reported that 90 per cent of murderers are male. Women get angry, they shout and they scream and have indeed even been known to kill false lovers and husbands, as well as batter their children, but according to statistics they do not often perform premeditated acts of violence – and yet it is to women's anger that we have given most attention over the last twenty years. Undoubtedly women are angry and they have always carried the blame for this problem. Men's angry behaviour has, however, been regarded as the norm.

So what then is this norm that Dr Miles refers to, particularly in the field of feelings? It is curiously depressing when, as these normal men open up to their fears, particularly their 90 per cent fear of humiliation and loss of face, which she says she finds linked closely to the way they see their manhood, it is hard for them to retain their honesty and handle their vulnerability.

Women play into the myth of men as creators or heroes and supermen, or powerful financial wizards, and they expect unrealistic things from their men. As women we need to love men as they are, and not from this mythological belief system, such as the one I was brought up with.

It is not that men are naturally violent – little boys are usually a lot more loving and sensitive to feelings than girls – but they get put through such a toughening-up process in childhood, as can be seen in our public school system. In the old days, rituals of manhood were – and still are – carried out in primitive parts of the world at puberty. Boys were flogged in public, and had to withstand days and nights alone in the wilderness, or were surrounded by wild animals. Too often in our society the notion of manhood is linked with pain. But to bear it manfully can lead to inflicting it on others.

Often in our personal relationships men do not hear what women say to them until it hurts them. Perhaps the fact that a vast percentage of divorces are initiated by women goes to prove this. Women warn, they plead to be heard, and as a last resort turn to divorce. What then happens to these hurt men? And to the generation of little boys torn between their father and mother, trying to behave in a 'normal' way?

Women will tend, says Dr Miles, to punish themselves more than men for their imperfections. There are more women with eating disorders than men for instance. Men become obsessed with their need to prove their manly strength and their manhood and in such situations they do it by inflicting violence in various ways, but usually on others rather than on themselves. These forms of violence include verbal cynicism, intellectualization and judgement, fighting and bullying and the recourse to sexual aids, including prostitution. All of these are about proving potency and power.

As fathers become included more in the care of their children, from being present at the birth onwards, they can help their sons to honour their emotions as much as they do their anatomical attributes, as well as to help eliminate all violence and bullying by recognizing it in school and sporting activities. This way it will no longer be a question of why do our boys become so aggressive, but rather the understanding that, given our beliefs about making boys into men, how can they avoid it?

We need to give our young generation of growing boys stimulating things to think about, that are not violent or aggressive.

In adult relationships, where the heart is closed and cannot express itself, we use sex as a substitute. It could be said then that sexual abuse is the need to abuse the other person for the despair in our own heart. Perhaps the moment of orgasm to many men – and maybe women too – allows the memory of

heartfelt feelings to emerge, and this is why so many relationships are so sexually orientated.

What then of those who are at this time choosing not to
marry and have children? Are they somehow preventing the
continuation of another generation of dysfunction? Are they
consciously or unconsciously struggling to change the DNA
genetic pattern they carry, by attempting to 'finish up' and
start anew? They may feel that they fail in not conforming to
society's norm, but now is not about conforming but about
beginning afresh; lighter, freer bodies represent lighter, freer
attitudes and produce lighter, freer mums!

SIXTEEN

FEAR AND ITS
MANY DISGUISES

It is necessary for each of us to know full well what is life-threatening and avoid or stick to it. Not allow ourselves to be pushed or persuaded to go over the edge.

I have always held a huge fear of therapists using such techniques as rebirthing, or 'rolfing' – anything which pushed me to my edge. When in my own time I re-experienced being almost still-born, with all its helplessness, I realized instantly how to have been taken to that edge by someone else before would have been too much. My instinct protected me: I would not have come back. Fear's danger signals get confused when we deny our intuition and suppress our fears. I have followed my own knowingness, hence that memory could surface and be re-experienced in its own time, at its own speed.

Another example of my unconscious frozen fear of not surviving near–death was drawn into my life – in the form of an earthquake. I was in Romania and its intensity was 6.5 on the Richter Scale. As I came out of sleep, I soon realized I was not on the night train to Scotland as I had thought! When in Bulgaria the same year, I found I had no visa to get out and a part of me knew I had to face my panic. Life always provides the perfect vehicle for experience; we have the choice to go through it or run away and double the feelings already trapped.

Many of us are locked in our fears. People are afraid of everything. They dare not risk living for fear of dying literally. We fear losing jobs, losing partners, money, position in society. We are afraid of success, or of being too happy, afraid to feel, or of change, and indeed of our own truth. Unreleased fear tightens the throat and neck and lower back (memories of preparing for action as in our birth), the shoulders rise, the knees lock (legs are our support system). Fear paralyses our life energy. We are so afraid of what we might lose that we cling helplessly to what we have and numb ourselves so as not to experience life, not to move forward. There is really no way out – life lives by its own rules despite what we do to control it and dam it up. Look at the seedling planted under the concrete paving – sooner or later it arrives on the surface. Life fulfils its fullest potential in all circumstances. If we free ourselves from our old anxieties, we can actually fear what we really need to fear.

During my 'earthquake' experience, I awoke to the rhythm of what I thought was the night train to Scotland. My body enjoyed the gentle rocking, until, as I became more conscious, my mind reminded me that this was Bucharest not Perth. I was not on a train but in my bedroom, and the whole building was moving. An earthquake! Suddenly every part of my being was wholly in the moment – my last? No, I was still alive. My first thought was the excitement of actually experiencing such a happening; my second, was how much my children would be impressed! My third was to get going quickly in case the building fell down. It all happened so fast, people pouring down the stairway – women in curlers crying, men in pyjamas and overcoats clutching half-open suitcases. And the inevitable American voice assuring us that all was under control. How did he know? No one helped anyone else – each was frozen in his own fear, yet as I had nothing by which to measure such an experience, I found that the fear came later.

I had taken my pillow and blankets and made a 'bed' among the shrubs outside, since in such a situation there is nowhere to go or run to in the world outside. I took a swig of Rescue Remedy and retreated inwards to that centre of stillness, surrendering. What would happen . . .? I had a great feeling of trust in that surrender – as if a part of me already knew it would be okay. Anyway, I was powerless to change events. I lay down under the stars, still feeling the earth's movements under my body and wondered what part this experience was playing in the larger picture of my life.

For one minute – that is all it lasted – I was brought to the gates of that great transition from life here to life there, through death. Why me? What for? This massive tremor that shook the earth, was it also my own earthquake, shifting parts of myself that would never again be the same, facing myself with all its fears?

My body gradually steadied and adjusted to the shock that comes with such an experience. I began the re-living of the evening before, that had led up to the earthquake. How around five p.m. after weeks of heat, quite suddenly a gale began to rise out of nowhere. The trees tossed and bent unnaturally in their endeavour to resist the wind's force. The rain came, driving against the windows, as if to break them. My mind flipped to Daphne Du Maurier's work *The Birds* and her description of the swarm of birds beating the windows – the noise!

I had stood at the window revelling in the sweet smell the rain had brought, enjoying the wildness of the wind and lightning that followed, illuminating the whole earth as it flashed. How I had enjoyed snuggling under the pretty red Romanian blankets on the first night that was destined not to be hot and stuffy. Then I re-lived the moment: my shock on every level as the fear cascaded through my body, relief at being alive; at the same time marvelling at the fine line we live so unconsciously between death and life held in here by a tack – as the old Scottish fisherman said to me after coming through a particularly hard winter!

This experience had done something extraordinary in fixing me to the Earth – even my commitment seemed stronger. The structure around fear of dying had indeed been loosened.

There is no fear in love, only in opening the heart to it. Fear leads us to act in desperation or to give in to despair.

SEVENTEEN

RELATIONSHIPS

The main value of relationships is to allow us to live at a tangible level that which at a deeper unconscious level is not yet ready to be seen. To be a victim of low self-esteem means that much of our energy is used in an attempt to deny what it is that we are ashamed of from our peers. This gives us very little freedom to be ourselves when with others; we over-identify with those we think much of. Within ourselves is deep depression and self-loathing. What a load to go out to dinner with! It all separates us from who we really are!

In three out of four of my relationships, I have chosen men who, as my father did, disappeared without explanation, leaving me with feelings of bewilderment, shame for not being enough, and very great pain in never being able to know what really was the reason for departure. They probably didn't either, then. Now I feel it is different. The break-up of my first marriage caused me to experience shock and outrage, on a very physical level, which I stifled into unconsciousness to cover my pride, to numb the pain and anger and survive the shame. I did it well, and like my mother herself had done before me, I 'coped'!

My second marriage and its ultimate end brought back the latent fear of being totally annihilated out of existence. I feared for my life and by going to that edge again, this time more emotionally and deeper than before, I initiated the necessary breach to survive once again. I took control! Looking back, had I dared let go and trusted my life to that man, it could well have been another way through, but at the time to trust a man with my life felt like suicide. Now I believe my second husband would have been willing to support me through near-death if he had known how. But instead, in his fear he was constantly absent, and I interpreted this as abandonment. How often does this happen in the break-up of our marriages?

Freud said that finding work and love are the two fundamental essentials in anyone's life. We deem ourselves ready for that lifelong commitment, often without having resolved the lessons of the earlier stages. In my own case I was not even aware they were there, let alone unsolved. I had to live through two marriages and the birth of three children before I really began to know how much of my relationship was about myself.

The third relationship was more in the nature of therapy than a mature relationship. I learned it was safe to live life and that I was not all the things I had had dumped on me and I had then believed. When I thought I knew myself enough to marry again, I gave my heart and my soul and my trust in my fourth relationship. With an absent father we give all of ourselves and lose all of ourselves, or do not give at all – there is no balance. And, as you know, I was abandoned but I had heard my inner message 'for the last time'.

My mother was a woman suddenly cut off from the man she loved and with whom she had had two children, who was also her financial and emotional security, to whom she looked for Life itself. Now she had to find it within herself. Marriage had brought Mama into authority over my father's household, and imbued her with a sense of her own identity as part of him; then suddenly she was alone and once again having to endure the sense of no identity. Today I understand her struggle much more and appreciate the reasons for the resentment I felt as a child – her lack of closeness which I now see for what it was – and on her death I grieved deeply for the loss of our relationship. In releasing the loss I have gained great strength.

This was the same pattern that I myself followed many years later. In 1989, the year that she died, I remember using the same metaphor when abandoned by the man I loved so dearly. 'But you are my life,' I said. 'You must think of it as a death,' he answered and bang – everything collapsed in the shock. Another death was one too many. So traumatic was that shock that somehow I knew it had to be about more than just the present.

The vicious circle of social pride, narrow-mindedness and control gets under way. 'Marriage' is the name our society gives to these unloving dysfunctional relationships. Perhaps the next generation can turn inwards, to face the wound of what they do not love rather than repeat its re-creation through further relationships – the quality of relating changes then. I doubt if I could have done differently, yet these are different times, and we are now learning that the focus of our suffering can become the force of our vitality.

The wound of the unloved comes to the surface when we are knotted up with another person. Such oneness and sharing is wonderful, yet the wound each time goes deeper, until the ultimate hidden first memory emerges. What is activated in anyone in the present has happened in the past, as far back as that pattern goes. It is like pressing a bell that sounds throughout the house. When a love affair ends abruptly this cut-off has happened before: a mother's shock during pregnancy or an unwanted child; the barren woman in her unconscious denial of her womanliness; or as in my case, to my father's declaring his certainty that I was a boy when in fact I was not; or my mother's fear of her pregnancy. I was fifty-three before I let go of that memory, trapped in the front of my left shoulder.

The way we were not loved in childhood can be read precisely from our later relationships. If we listen to each other we can help each other. We can mirror for each other in our closeness the blind spots – the unloved areas, the places we don't see clearly in ourselves – and then support each other to face them within the closeness, instead of feeling alone and abandoned.

The emotionally repressed, unloved young man always seeks his mother in his lover, longing for the eyes to reflect the love he never had. What happens when he finds it? Alas, he becomes emotionally dependent and is incapable of seeing and feeling that partner as a separate individual. He then panics at his dependency and in his fear of being controlled and smothered as he nearly was in childhood, plus his other fear of abandonment – he rejects the love he's given by being totally caught up in his memory of being unloved. In this desperate state, and in an attempt to end the emotional struggle, he will look for a controlling intellectual woman and marry her. Two years of incubation time passes, and what does he find but that his controlling 'mate' is denying her feelings for fear of her anger at being unloved, which will simply serve to prod him at a deeper level. His denial will then unleash her anger. I suspect I came very near to such a marriage that last time.

When we break up and lose someone we love, it is as if for a time we lose our soul and experience the hole, and before we have the willingness to go through the hole and onwards there is a 'frozen-ness' about our connection to life – very often manifesting physically in our breathing. As long as our heart is set on the one we have lost, the one we cannot have, the hopeless feeling of being powerless to do anything overtakes us and there is an impasse with no way forward. Again and again we return to this place, to freeze it, deaden it and pretend to ourselves we have come through it – or follow the experience through to freedom, experiencing a living death to know that we need not die as we almost did – but a lot of this comes on rebirth.

Our loneliness, then, is an unfulfilled desire for intimacy. When I entered into solitude, I was confronted by it with its unrelenting pain and desperation. In accepting being with it, I understood why so many live lives of 'quiet desperation' with no confrontation. I learned about my own human-ness – my vulnerability when tested: I was kneaded, wrecked, tossed relentlessly by the pain, but I also experienced insights and understanding into the human condition previously unimagined, realizing that my loneliness was that of all mankind. This was the only way home – to keep with the pain, the guilt, the anger, watching the understanding and enlightenment it was 'giving birth' to within me. Rather than separating from my dying, I walked hand in hand with it, with the awareness of the underlying rebirth of sureness, love, and the vision and knowing of the expanded feeling of joy and freedom that lay ahead – my own crucifixion of myself. I accepted my utter human-ness in the feeling of aloneness and abandonment; until the resurrection and new beginning, this time with a love and an understanding that had a whole other dimension – that of my soul – of knowing for sure that all was right in the world and in me, exactly as it was.

Our 'pain', then, can produce a deep, unshakable strength –
the loneliness and loss can become a love that appears to
embrace all. There can be a peace and serenity – and the
knowing that all things are possible.

When I stand on top of a hill and see clearly all around, I feel
this; but when I come down into the valley and lose the overall
view, I forget the intensity of what I have experienced. Life has
its cycles: a beginning, a middle and an end. Like the tide, we
have a going-in phase, a phase of solitude and reflection, only
to return again outwards, like a dance. We may be at a point
of going-in to experience the aloneness, the pain and solitude
through which we reach new understanding. At this point I
felt incapable of loving another and afraid of opening my own
heart for fear of pain – and so ran away. I was safe in my
withdrawal.

I must again risk, challenge, confront that barrier, that
frozen-ness of my solitary state; to find, as Goethe says, 'All
manner of unforeseen things occurring', and all things seeming
possible again. The heart feeling stronger, the door from solitude opening and a different aloneness and feeling of power
beginning to well up. My heart is no longer weak, scared and
ineffectual, timid and untrustworthy. I have moved from the
place of fear, feeling frozen and trapped in something greater
than me, 'longing' to, but unable to move through it, to finding
the opening and strength to go through.

Now I am ready to return to my human-ness and to others.
The journey now takes a different direction: I have experienced the silence, solitude and loneliness and having
re-established the ability to relate to myself, I can turn
towards my brothers and sisters in time, space and matter.

The unfolding stages within our relationships, from trust
through betrayal to forgiveness, are a movement of consciousness. For all its negativity, betrayal is still an advance over
trust since it leads to death of the power of control through the
experience of suffering, and if this is not *blocked* by revenge,
denial, cynicism or self-betrayal, it becomes a journey of a
reconciliation to ourselves.

Whatever my strides of advancement I am still human, not
perfect! Still vulnerable and unsure, but very much more at
ease and more aware of the struggles of others as they touch

what threatens their ability to remain here on earth; as I have touched my own.

In the third relationship that I have described I had all the possibilities of genuine happiness, yet I could not settle for that; the journey to myself had not ended yet, the cycle was still incomplete. Here was an opportunity to feel considerably 'more' yet still I felt 'less'. I was still not aware of why. In the final relationship as I have explained earlier, I was more conscious of who I was; my confidence in having a value had been won in these healing, strengthening years, and I was ready as I thought to wed with my shining knight in his wig – his courting me with such dedication convincing me that here was where true happiness lay.

In reality the Judge replayed my father's doting love for me and, having given to me in abundance, he panicked and ran. He feared his own truth and the changes. Caught in the rules he had set for himself, he gave in to sabotaging all he had so longed for in favour of suppression. He certainly made me feel more, yet the pain he saw in me, the dependency of the child I did not know in myself and that he did not want to know in himself – was just too much for him. While he feared to go out to his edge, I on the other hand was now ready to complete the journey to myself, begun unconsciously so early in gestation.

I can see now that just as we experience dependency when we are babies, we look for it again in our relationships. In the first moments of birth, as in the first moments of a relationship, we experience freedom. Then the rage at finding ourselves helpless, dependent and apparently trapped sets in. In order to heal these very beginnings, we re-enact out through our relationships those early days, again and again, until our relating becomes interdependency instead of the child's dependency. My dependency was less of a threat to the Judge than the fear of being abandoned by me, and this drove him to the understandable panic and subsequent betrayal.

In re-experiencing my early days I became aware that in order to have a value and be recognized as the first-born in my family it was necessary to be a boy and to carry on the title. I complied with neither. In my re-experience of those early weeks of gestation and subsequent birth, I was astonished to be able to feel the high degree of resentment I felt towards my parents' unconscious wishes, and later towards my mother for her disinclination to use her title. My resentment stemmed from her having, and not using, one of the things I needed to validate myself within the unconscious family belief system, which I felt I needed for my survival.

When young, we learn to feel about ourselves through the adults around us. We implicitly trust what we feel. As we grow, we recreate over and over again this emotional environment from our early years; unconsciously victims of these circumstances until, as adults and not children, we can choose our lives, not as dependent victims but with freedom of choice.

Many of us become self-sufficient and controlling – through fear of hurt – and in this there is anger and the separation from (instead of integration with) the child within us. This, if freedom to live is to be reached, we must return to release.

How useful it would be if by burying the past we could be finished with it, but alas, it cannot be so. This way we only separate from it, and although this may be an expedient way of coping with what is too difficult to deal with at the time (as it was for the Judge), it was not for me, and by breaking away in the violent way he did he caused my lifeline to be very severely tested. This can result in death, as I now know, which would mean gathering the strength and courage to face again the same cycle to arrive at the same place of experience.

Now that there are those who themselves have consciously re-experienced this 'life-death' or preconception place of choice and know it is exactly that – a choice to die or live, an opportunity to release what is nearly dead – therapy has extended beyond techniques.

If in one of my sessions I have someone who says they want to die, I seldom find this is what they really mean; rather that they do not know how to live through the acute feelings and survive. So I will agree to journey with them, knowing from my own journey just how necessary it is to live out the terror and dread of that place, and to reach the realization that where I thought there was death, there is – but there is the option of life through the dying to the frozen part of myself. Do the journey fully and consciously and it is not necessary to return.

Although the climb back is a long one I felt as if for years and years I had been submerged like a submarine, and to float to the top and experience the rightness of being alive brought such joy and freedom I could, to begin with, hardly bear it.

At the end of a relationship how important it is to wean each other gradually and with clear and honest communication, without cutting, as it were, the 'lifeline' of the one left alone. I have worked with men and women who have become impotent through such shock, and one woman whose right heel was unable to touch the ground in her fear of standing alone. Our gentle support for one another gets lost in the possible fear of being trapped, the old memories again of that child that could not get away!

The way I coped in extreme shock was to leave my body, but people react in many different ways. One of my clients, Sarah, for instance, all but fell on to the chair in my workroom between the heavy sighs and tears that ran down her face. 'I feel as heavy as sin,' she said to me. 'My heart feels like it's been pierced by a dagger. I'm feeling panicky, but I'm angry and feel as though I've been abused. I feel as if my trust has been broken. My dreams have been crushed, my pain denied recognition. I am confused and bewildered by what I haven't done, yet there must be something. It's as if my womanhood has been smashed. My identity as Sarah has been annihilated and nobody hears me. I just want to numb what's happening in case it's too much to bear. My marriage is over. He's disappeared and refuses communication.' To survive this experience she had removed herself to a place outside her body; so that there was a sense of haziness and non-reality, as I described in my own experience of feeling like Ophelia – of 'floating', with no legs.

When we looked at what had happened earlier in Sarah's life, it was one long history of loss. So this situation, as in my own, was traumatic enough in the way it was done, not in the fact that her husband left, but how. All her fuses blew at once. She was holding on by a thread. So together we stayed with total awareness, in that place where her lifeline was struggling and gradually over the next few weeks the terror began to subside and give way to dread and shame, as the old outdated family patterns emerged. Her husband in his fear and guilt could not bring himself to make any contact, and in a way it was like a death for Sarah. There was no 'goodbye'. No time to ask the questions that needed to be asked, and to hear the other's truth. Alone, it is infinitely harder to cut the ties. This is where I feel we act with unnecessary harshness to each other, and with unnecessary lack of charity. Whatever the cost – communicate!

If it is impossible for the couple to talk to each other without too much emotion then a third person can be helpful, even if they say very little. Above all, healing is necessary and cannot be done purely alone – there are psychic ties that remain tied even when someone has died. If that someone is still alive to forgive and be forgiven, it is so vital to our future, and future relationships to cut the ties that bind. It is the only way to be completely free – yet how many of us do it?

As we reach a degree of emotional maturity through our journey to ourselves, so interdependency emerges, and we can remain loving with a much greater degree of trust in the other without the need or wish to change them, or separate from what we see and do not like. Within the laws of the Universe we are all creators in our own right.

Our life and relationships work to the extent that we can accept and forgive what we judge in ourselves as unlovable. We create every dis-ease within us; which will manifest roughly two years later in some way in the physical body.

The examples of abandonment and worthlessness were lived out in each of my four relationships in different ways, until finally, in going beyond the protective layers of myself, into the finer being of myself – into what David Bohm refers to as the immaculate, that which is beyond body and mind into the resonant beingness of oneself – where I was inwardly shattered by the new understanding of all being related to all. I realized how we sclerose ourselves in personal emotion and now I could see beyond that, I could feel the dynamics of life as I touched the soul's emotions. I perceived through the anger to its deepest dimension of outrage – no longer in a personal way, but to the motion of the universe and then beyond this again to the immaculate place. Watching all these layers I experienced all this as a process of the releasing of frozen energy in near-death trauma. In choosing life, I understood the meaning behind the feelings of abandonment and betrayal.

In our longing for purity and unconditional love, the sacred in us takes us into relationships where it gets tarnished; we get hurt, and our vision of the immaculate that we see in the other gets lost – we do not trust it any more. In returning and reconnecting to this state of being, we give the opportunity for another to do the same by our lightness of being. Through our living of life hand in hand with joy.

But what makes us feel not good enough? To separate from this unworthy part of ourselves makes us dependent on another or others for our emotional stability. We *all* carry this memory of inadequacy since we came through parents who unconsciously carried it and felt the same sense of not being good enough. Acceptance and healing ourselves leads to our *own* integration and freedom from dependency on others, and also to our own emotional maturing.

What limits us from throwing out things within ourselves as we would in spring-cleaning a room? Do we not want to see and own our own untidiness? A part of us may be afraid of what we think we might find, as in my birth as a girl and not the much-awaited son – or as with my mother whom I came through, and who was also very fearful and well-filled with pain-killing drugs. How did I, the baby remember this? Quite simply I gave up trying, gave up my instinctive urge to follow life forward in my inability to get down the birth canal, I gave up the pointless effort. So, up until my near-death experience I lived my life with a belief of hopelessness in ever achieving anything – and the rejection at birth for being a girl reinforced the hopelessness. Although the huge fight to make it into the world possibly gave me my strong will. I passed this will on to my second daughter, who needed it for her own life struggle.

The whole experience was made unconsciously fuzzy by the drugs given to my mother. I came into this life in a state of 'bewilderment', only to feel the fear around me that mounted to panic as the doctor realized that I was almost dead. I was so unable to breathe, that my state was not conducive to moving out into life. The fact of not breathing was probably frozen in panic in my chest and I was fifty years old before I experienced any malfunction with my own breathing, yet all my three children had weaknesses in their chests, as did two of my four partners. What we cannot yet touch within ourselves, we attract through another and live in close proximity to, in order one day to draw to the surface that which is yet unconscious within ourselves.

In the final relationship my partner had had TB. The early 'pain' in the heart and lung had also physically manifested in his lower left leg and, due to surgery there, later in the lower back. Whereas my first husband and children had manifested a mild form of bronchitis, it was this last manifestation of the dis-ease behind TB that forced my own dis-ease to the surface. I had to re-establish my connection to life with my body and 'be here'. The risk I took in shaking my foundations meant a whole rebuilding process. If our memories are held in different areas of the body, and can manifest in dis-ease, then what we can transform of our past creates a freer and more alive present and future for us.

The necessary 'spring cleaning' of the early years helps us to realize that, just as we could not have acted differently, given that same situation, same awareness, emotional state and so on, this was also true for our parents. If we blame, deny or turn our backs on life, it is a sure way to stay stuck in a problem.

To blame another is to make someone else responsible for how I feel and to give away my power to alter my life dependency. As we look back to our parents' childhoods, we begin to notice the patterns that continue down through a family, each generation playing it out differently. We can try to feel how it was to be them: photographs can help you to enter into a person and feel their feelings and so understand their strengths and weaknesses. You can also do this with childhood pictures of yourself. Understanding leads to acceptance, and acceptance to love and forgiveness, and so freedom to live with easy interdependency instead of uneasy dependency.

We all have ability to transform our limitations. To go back and forgive the child in us that has struggled to adulthood through such early limited beliefs as have described requires courage and perseverance in facing the pain. As a child we cannot choose, we are bound by 'them' – the adults – and their attitudes, feelings and behaviour patterns. As adults we can choose to do it 'my way', to remember the beauty of loving life, of trusting life from way back before birth and to again live life with that quality. A sense of joy wells up and expresses itself in the light and order and shininess of a room well spring cleaned, a sense of peace and deep achievement reigns. That can be true for us too. It is enough to be who I am, then what I believe can come true.

Another viewpoint is that we unconsciously invite people into our lives because of what they reflect; to get a private view of both our darker and lighter sides. In our relationships there are times when we lose sight of ourselves – sometimes it is too confronting to own and mostly it is easier to hate and blame another for what we do not want to see in ourselves, but they cannot do the job for us. When only a bomb can shift the fixed state of our consciousness, or take us to the edge of our earthly lives, then somehow we invite just such relations into our lives. Or dis-ease and death in our children.

In each of my relationships I could see in the other an unknown part of myself and was drawn to it. We are drawn together in the hope of sharing the other's life. The new life that each sees in the other is like death to the life that up until now has been familiar. We enter into friendship but our friendship is not based on sharing a life that is familiar, like two people who live within the same world. Rather it is based on sharing an unknown life, a life beyond the familiar. Each is linked through the other to an unknown world as yet dormant within. No doubt the life one finds in another is the life one lacks, so we bring to the meeting the other one's own lack, and the image we form of each other is 'fulfilment'. In knowing the other, we come to understand our lack, as I have, and the other does open up the way to fulfilment, but we have to tread the path to claim the lack.

If the relationship splits, or one or the other dies, the feeling for the one that is left is that of death, of being cut off from all that is safe and familiar. As long as another person is one's only link to a new and unknown life one does not yet live the new life oneself, one is joined to it and yet separated from it. Marriage is being linked through another to the new life. Marriage of oneself with oneself would be living the new life oneself. If one is unwilling to be alone, one dwells only in the human circle. If unwilling to be in need, one dwells in solitude. If one is willing to live both, there is fullness through and beyond the loss of the beloved, and the journey to oneself is completed.

Just as women in their relationship to themselves become one with their womanliness, both the beautiful and the ugly, and can rejoice in both, so men can experience these aspects of themselves within themselves and without fear.

Women can draw men into themselves to experience their depths, as men can draw women out into their worldliness. The tree's strength and beauty depends much on the depth of its roots. Our human strength for both sexes depends on our firm connection to the Earth. Our pain forces our barriers and dissolves our brick walls, and is often, alas, the only way we learn and move forward.

Spiritual needs and human needs are found in different spheres. Perhaps spiritual needs come to be met through human relationships in that the relationship takes us to the edge of our aloneness, our emptiness, our need. At this point the journey moves to within; and then, through the longing for answers, it becomes possible on the return journey out again to relate to others out of more fullness than before, and to touch our love for all life. I do feel this.

As long as another person represents my soul or the desire in my heart then I have not yet built it for myself within my own heart and cannot love another with all my heart. Through loss and betrayal we can find, and claim back, that soul quality. Only *then* can we willingly let go the other and become capable of loving with our heart and soul, because our love is unconditional, not restricted. Our love then becomes the love of God and, trusting that, we can love another.

It might seem that we are programmed not for life and living, but rather for woe and burden and pain. Not for trust and openness and honest communication together, but rather in hiding and pretending and never reaching our potential state of joy and freedom as human beings. Do we live in 'boxes' with labels on the doors and enter each other's box only through the door alone, forgetting there may be other ways to explore? Things are changing as the old structures give way, and the rules of the past we find no longer apply to our present lives. All over the world people are on the move. The Berlin Walls are crumbling between nations, races, relationships and class structures, and individuals are discovering their sameness, where before we related with barriers of differences.

EIGHTEEN

RELEASING THE OLD
FEARS THROUGH THE
NEXT GENERATION

ANOREXIA

Anorexia is about withdrawal – withdrawal to the point, as my second daughter H.M.C. said, that 'I am so far above the clouds I cannot even see or sense any longer where that might be'. Fear and panic in children's lives, I am now sure, lie beneath their rejection of people and the outside world.

There are two approaches to break through that separation:

1. to break the will and make that individual respond;
2. to honour the innate intelligence within that person and their need to withdraw; and to endeavour to understand why.

I remember asking H.M.C. how I could help her, as she would have to make her decision to live or die, and she said, 'By keeping away'. I remember my terror that she might die and my outrage at what she asked – 'What would people say?' But I did it. I accepted that it was her decision to be anorexic; it was her timing and probably the only way she could transform her own living death which now, I know, went much further back to her father's leaving us before she was born; and the shock that was so life-threatening for me (remembering the patterns) was also, through my body, threatening hers (but that re-interpretation was of not being wanted by me).

Over the subsequent years, many further understandings have come to light, one of which was: could her father's leaving mean that she was not his child? This, as she said, had the flaw in it that she looked so exactly like him.

H.M.C. touched near-death three times that I know of and, with her remarkable wisdom, I hope she will one day write her own story to help those who travel that narrow tightrope between life and death.

What I uncovered as I faced my fear and anger was a pattern of worthlessness going back another two generations at least. As I loosened the structure of my own past during the next few years, so my daughter was able to grow stronger and feel safer, having less need to separate from her body, her family and, therefore, life on Earth.

It has been a wholly challenging and quite extraordinary journey; it has had its moments of fun and laughter, as it has had its moments of struggle. I am certain we have loosened, if not transformed, the pattern of worthlessness and of denial of the feminine principle of belief that ran through the women in my mother's family, all of whom had an abundance of unex-pressed talent. The men on the other hand harnessed and used theirs with much less difficulty. Is this the beginning of the end of a pattern in which, for us women, it is easier to deny or die than to step out and claim?

If we can help the will to be here, we can come through the fear of not surviving. H.M.C. and I have shared many of our discoveries and each time, although it was harder for her to put her experience into words, we came up with the same conclusions.

From the time that anorexia became more openly acknowl-edged – around 1975 – I instinctively knew that of my three children H.M.C. would be the one to walk that path if any of them did – so I knew she was unconsciously choosing anorexia before it became obvious in her body. The shock of her father's leaving created in me the despair of being trapped with two children, unable to reach him as he was abroad with his regiment, and leaving me to care for and feed them, because, on learning that she was not going abroad as plan-ned, the nanny also left! I would today, however, call my 'caring' abuse, since that is what it was: how could I, with all this taking place, give to my little daughter anything but a deep sense of worthlessness?

Some years later she said how sorry and sad she was for

giving me so much heartache, and I remember saying,
'Oh, but I have learnt so much by this experience and from
you.'

'That's just the decision I remember making at the time I
became anorexic,' she replied. 'They must learn.'

How differently she saw things from the way I had thought
she did. How much of myself I saw in her.

Many of us commonly fear to feel too much in case we are
overwhelmed. But this is actually only our idea of how we will
cope with our feelings. In our own time we can come through
the pain and terror of stored memories, even if they seem very
life-threatening. By giving ourselves the necessary permission
to go to that place where death is a choice, we probably will
not need to die but will, instead, melt the cemented 'anorexic'
part of ourselves that is waiting, shrivelled and cold, for our
loving act of release.

H.M.C.'s anorexia set in at the age of puberty. Now aged
twenty-eight she has her own home, but when she was preparing to move there, the old fear returned. I suggested we
could try some work together and she willingly agreed –
something that before she would have been more hesitant to
do. Later, she wrote about this decision as follows:

> I think we both knew, subconsciously, that it was a time of make
> or break in the *serious* sense of the phrase; Mum reached out and I
> took that 'hand' without even having to think (which I have to
> over practically EVERYTHING) – the time was right I guess and
> so it turned out IT WAS RIGHT perhaps it was REALLY the
> beginning of the end of a life time of purgatory for me – to begin
> to understand and feel those first moments of my existence, to
> then set me free to BE *myself* in my life which, had I had my
> choice, I would not have entered.
>
> So it was, I took Mum's 'hand' and I took her help in the
> form that she has now learned to give it to others – in a non-
> demanding, non-judgemental and unconditional form – so dif-
> ferent from those other times she may have reached out to me in
> the past.
>
> There was no second thought, the timing was right though in
> no way calculated by either of us, I feel; we've both fought so
> hard and for so long neither of us want to die now, yet a break
> between mother and daughter HAS to be a kind of death for both
> parties does it not? At birth – at adulthood.

Again my life was threatened, as I 'prepared for action' to move house.

It was not until the third session that the real breakthrough happened though – at that time I was suffering from the recurring symptom of VERY swollen jaw glands which NO ONE from Orthodox/Alternative medicine could explain – and all I knew was that when they were bad they ONLY dispersed when I vomited.

I learned during this third session that Mum WILLED me to be born on 5.1.63 for other family reasons *she* had decided *for* me – I was to be born then, and SO I WAS . . . but effectively what happened was SHE MADE ME ENTER THIS WORLD in HER TIMING and I was not ready or ALLOWED TO CHOOSE FOR MYSELF; I believe that actually had Mum not got me here through her will I would not have come at all or I would have been stillborn – had it been left to MY choice.

So, ALL MY LIFE I have had this BURNING resentment towards Mum, stemming from – I was not sure where and this DRIVE to do things BY myself, WHEN and HOW I wanted to. I was striving to be allowed to do things in my own timing when I felt it was right to do them; subconsciously I think I felt had been forced once to go against my own timing – therefore there was no chance of me ever allowing this to happen again. Mum asked what I was getting rid of when I vomited – answer = fear and anger. Let that go – you don't need to vomit to get rid of that, just let it go right down into you and through you, Mum said. I visualized just that and I felt the slimy substance in my glands begin to OOZE out into my mouth, and down and through me. This acrid, sour burning taste began to seep through my system – which I felt was just POISON. You could say fear/anger *is* poison.

That happened, during the session, and continued on through the afternoon of that day; within 24 hours my glands were normal again though the following day my stomach was like water and the day after that I felt VERY tired.

I have now come through two very major traumas since then with no recurrence of *having* to vomit OR swollen glands; I have to remember sometimes not to clench my jaw or grind my teeth but now I KNOW when I am doing it – before I did not and even if I did I didn't know how much pain, fear and anger I was hanging on to through doing it. I ALSO no longer wake up in the night grinding my teeth!

I do believe this is the beginning of the end for the *need* for numbness and pain for me – Mum reached out, I *allowed* her in, she was able to help me and I accepted that help; is this not the purpose of and what TRUE *friends* [and support] are about now today and in the future?

MAKING IT BETTER

In relating what my second daughter, H.M.C., went through, I don't want you to imagine that because my eldest daughter, A.L., was a different character she avoided her share of trauma – she didn't. She was three when her father, and then the nanny, left. She it was who watched my mother replay her unexpressed grief at my father's death, as my husband left me. She 'saw' all my pain and chose unconsciously to be the family's 'carer', forgetting for many years to care for her own needs by imprisoning herself in the needs of others.

She became for us like Amelia Ann (without the curlers!) in those wonderful books about a large family of children; always doing everything to please, and doing it so well and so willingly that no one noticed the frightened little girl deep inside who felt so lost and unsupported. Her teen years were a bit untidy and the tea towel would wing its way through the air across the kitchen in my direction with such phrases as 'You do your own drying up; I am not your servant'. Then there was her wobbly decision at seventeen to move in with her boyfriend, delivered to me on Ascot station en route for the Convent where my youngest daughter (the only Catholic) had started school and stood in her rather too-long navy tunic, with holy medallions around her neck and teddy clasped in her arm, all of ten years old, eyes and ears and mouth aghast at what her eldest sister was proposing. For her anything A.L. did was tinged with perfection, but not this time. The nuns would not handle this with loving understanding.

The train was in the station for three minutes and I knew I only had that time to sow any delicate seed of wisdom I could muster up. If nothing else, I could get her to forestall the decision until at least daughter number three was safely up the drive with the nuns once more, by which time I hoped God in His infinite mercy might have had a word in A.L.'s ear too. After much discussion it was agreed she would spend the weekends with the boyfriend and the week with my mother, which as it turned out was just as well, since that particular liaison died its natural death a month or two later!

A.L. learnt to understand her imprisonment of herself by working with those who were either homeless, or unwanted. At university she looked after a family of five children fostered by two families in the same town, in order that they could remain near each other. Later in London she spent Thursday evenings helping those from ethnic families in a youth club. I remember her saying how the only approach was one of no approach, but of waiting until these children that had least of all trust in others, could open the door to communication. Later when living in Peru she visited the prison there, and was the negotiator of the subsequent release of one of the inmates. Now in her late twenties I see her putting her own 'caring' and needs before those of the world which makes me very happy. She has chosen to make her home back in Scotland.

So each of us, as you see, has imprisoned our fears and our pain. I in my disease of rheumatoid arthritis, one daughter in anorexia and the other in taking over my role as Mummy and caring for us all. It's interesting to note that the patterns are also there with my third daughter, although she has a different father and is much younger, and so now the patterns are differently arranged, nearly thirty years later, in a much looser structure. At such a young age what was still unconscious for me is conscious for S.C. as number 3, and already she makes very clear choices about her life without having to go through the same hoops that I did. For her it seems that thought and the action are much closer together.

I feel so blessed to have them as my companions in this lifetime. Their laughter, support and wisdom have helped me in my journey to my self. Without them I might not have pulled through.

PART THREE

Conscious Ease and Transformation

NINETEEN

BEYOND THERAPY

I can see a picture of myself as a child climbing a stile, with the grown-ups pacing on ahead, talking and laughing and forgetting that there's a little person, crying out with an outstretched hand, wanting to climb over but not able to because she does not know how. The adult in us has the choice to hear the child and walk back and help, or to walk on and try to drown its crying by talking and laughing and ignoring with the other adults. I was ready to claim my abandoned child.

I was talking more now of my journey through dis-ease. I can honestly say that in my work I never meet an illness or a broken bone that is not entirely representative of whatever the person (however unconsciously) is struggling to make sense of within themselves. I can help people to hear (what they already unconsciously know) to the extent that they are ready to hear. Some people make huge changes almost instantly, others take months or years. Some completely resist and freeze in denial, remaining stuck in limbo for fear of altering the situation. I see others, however, who choose to face the kind of risks that would be honoured with a VC decoration were they in military service. The choice is commitment to responsibility, or pretending that everything is fine.

My own process has been with therapists and teachers from all over the world, who have always turned up in my life at just the right time. 'Trust the process' is the motto. If something feels right, I do it; had I merely thought about some of the choices I have made I would not have had the courage to make them. These were the hardest lessons, yet always the most valuable. My journey has taken me further and further into myself to create a solid foundation through its very unravelling. That cycle seems to be in completion through writing this book.

I am immensely grateful for both the people and the opportunities that have helped me to clear what feels like many generations of congealed soot in an old chimney, manifesting itself in my physical body as rheumatoid arthritis and in my emotional body as rheumatic fever.

Today I am free of pain. I feel ten tons lighter, I can trust the Earth and my feet on it; I begin to know and acknowledge the immense abundance of energy and wisdom that exists everywhere for us to draw on; and I know that in being gentle with myself and listening deep inside I get to where I need to be, and do what I need to do, with so much less expenditure of myself and my energy.

Life is now much more full of joy. Work has become play, and relaxation can be work. The different levels of myself now dance together where before they fought to control the whole of me. Of course, I still get caught playing the old records, old patterns, but as I move up on my own unfolding spiral of existence these patterns are experienced as from a different part of myself. When I meet that old knot I unravel it consciously – and walk on.

I see each of us as we climb our spiral, as our energies become less heavy and the current is transformed in our electrical circuits, raising the collective voltage for our countries and their special consciousness. (For Scotland, I feel it is the drawing of these depths of Universal Knowledge up and out of the symbolic squares and rectangles to be found in the Scottish tartan: the structure of the square represents the ego self requiring that the mould be broken.) As this happens, each country's collective 'electricity' will join the whole of human consciousness moving on to another and finer level in balance with other planets – our brothers and sisters in the Galaxy, the Cosmos, the Infinite.

There is a part of all of us that I am sure is limitless but to be so, we have to believe it and be ready for the responsibility it brings, of being limitless within the limitations of our humanity. So dare we risk? Perhaps at best the only choice for our human species is to go forward or resist. 'Movement is Life', Moshe Feldenkrais would say, 'and to live life without movement is unthinkable, a slow death.'

The future comes out of the here-and-now; I live and breathe in this moment as my doings today become my success or failures of tomorrow. Yesterday has gone, and with it all that was yesterday; a cycle completed. Today I carry only what I choose to carry of those memories, strengths and weaknesses. Every moment can be a point of choice in us, to carry on with the old patterns, old beliefs, old traditions that no longer serve or enhance our lives or, as you read this, at this very moment, to choose to move on through and shed the inappropriate and out of date and 'buy something new' to go forward with; to give yourself a gift in this very moment to help your life live!

Whatever your life and responsibilities, you can choose to do this. If you need help with it these days there are many many people who will give you a hand over your stile. 'Ask' said Jesus, 'and it shall be given unto you'; dare to ask, knowing that the help is there. To ask while still 'knowing' that we are not worthy to receive never works. The self-imposed unworthiness negates the asking.

My 1986 visit to Bulgaria allowed me to experience the restrictions of the Communist system and the effect that it had on both the inner and the outer lives of those I met. I remember returning to my home in the Scottish hills with feelings of such joy and gratitude for that freedom just 'to be' and that freedom to make choices. The tears rolled down my face, and for nights afterwards I would wake, stretching my body, and letting go of the unconscious tension that I had collected; feeling the escape of my spirit into Life again.

A part of my work today is involved in supporting, in whatever way I can, those people involved in building bridges between Eastern and Western Europe. What an enormous privilege it was to experience their lives, even for that short time. Finding myself in Bulgaria without a visa and in Romania in a fair-sized earthquake did somewhat heighten the experience.

Our species is indeed at the dawn of great changes and I see each of us, as we awake to that dawning, making the conscious choice either to move on with the Earth's 'spring-cleaning' that we can see all around us, understanding the need

for it and knowing that it leads to 'New Decoration'; or merely
seeing a mess that the world cannot get out of, and living in
blinkers. My sense is that people can only do the latter for a
while; as with any fear, it has to be faced in the end. As science
has now proved, our minds can travel into other minds, so at
some level of consciousness we are all one. That being so, we
can only move forward in consciousness 'as one'.

So now I am alone and testing myself with work and travel.
I find that to advertise is hopelessly unsuccessful, and yet
clients come, and one often leads to another. I have only ever
had two clients wanting me to be responsible for their lives in
the thirty years I have worked. I discovered I could travel and
buy my own ticket, and that I could lead groups with far more
ease than I imagined and actually enjoy it, and that much
could be done with humour.

THE HOUSE GROUP AT 'NO. 56'

I sold my family home a year or so after my separation from
my second husband and moved to London; found a delightful
house in a cul-de-sac and designated one floor as a drawing
room and small work room, the one below for the family
(with the garden) and the lower ground floor for my work. In
fact it didn't work out like that, because once my travelling
days began, others used the lower floor except for the Monday
nights' meditation.

This meditation started with just two of us. Each Monday
he would appear and ask where 'the others' were. Each Monday I would say no one else has come, but I thought it was a
test for our integrity; let us meditate and talk and see if at the
end he felt it had been a waste of his time. And each time he
would admit that in spite of his resistance to meditating without a group he had got what was appropriate that day. In time
a group did form but it was a huge test of my commitment and
self worth!

Curiously enough, once the group did form, the man with
whom I had originally begun it left. It was most rewarding
those Monday evenings and I noticed two particular things
happen. Firstly it was a large room, so there was space for

everyone. Secondly, there was the presence of a shepherd figurine that watched with us. When I moved the group meetings two floors up the shepherd did not come but instead young angelic beings were seen to keep us company. The downstairs room was green and gave a sense of peaceful homeliness. Upstairs the room was small and square and turquoise. People felt nearer to their problems and to each other and quite alarmed at the room's strength of energy to begin with. As we settled, we began to merge with it and some very moving and dynamic happenings took place. In 1982, I moved house and expanded the evenings into Open House soirees. Now in Wiltshire, they are Open House Days, held four times a year.

At that point, my dear friend Jill took the group to her home and continued with it there, weaving in her ways and her friends and their different influences to make it what it has become today with her guidance and warmth of character.

TWENTY

LIFE AS A CHALLENGE
NOT A THREAT

Space weaponry damages Earth's antennae.
Spirit is ever expanding.
Personality is ever-changing, limiting, judging, controlling.
A reverence for God or the essence of light is the foundation
   for all else.

'Don't fight the hills, laddie,' the Highlander will say. 'Be part
of them, make no effort, allow the hills to take you up. Give
time to resting the heart. Go steady. We tend to travel too fast
trying to prove.'

Life on earth is an inner personal journey manifested outwardly in our work, relationships and attitudes. Nothing
is very different in that respect from the generations before,
only our understanding through consciousness has changed.
In becoming less unconscious we 'lighten'. If we go further and become 'enlightened', can we change the need for
disease?
   'One thing you can't hide,' said John Lennon, 'is when you're
crippled inside'. There are, I feel sure, other dimensions of life
with which we can interact through thoughts; and the expansion of our minds. Can we reach out for such knowledge,
beyond time and matter, and bring it back into our daily lives,
thereby not restricting ourselves to the experience of one
dimension? We are powerful enough as beings but until now
we have been afraid to claim that power. To recognize and live

our multi-dimensionality instead of resisting or denying it, means we become effective in changing the quality of life all around us.

As we reach nearer and nearer to our own essence we evolve in the understanding that there can be no comparisons between us humans, no authoritarian figures, no greater or lesser; we are all 'light'. We can be a 'light' to draw others into their own light by reflection, and we can be our own light. This opens up unending possibilities. An atom is a light unto itself as well as a cell.

Behind the veil of no reality that the mind is busy maintaining, there is an aspect of creativity, as yet largely unconscious, and unexplored. Here, disease, accidents, ageing and death cannot be. This is energy, the light that is beyond all restraints of time, space and matter, and therefore beyond duality. If we can penetrate this core within, light realizes itself in us, releasing dis-ease completely.

The blueprint at the cellular level is there in unconsciousness. This was my childhood remembrance of oneness with colour, light and sound, touched on some fifty years ago. All things are possible!

Perhaps we must ask ourselves what then is new in this New Age of ours? A holistic approach is simply a variation on old modes, a gathering together of what was the past. Is it simply the quality of the life force energy that is changing?

We are, according to Gaston St Pierre, two distinct inputs of energy, which are nothing to do with the existing level of being in time, space and matter where the mind is in control. It is possible to take the consciousness or energy of out-of-time space and matter and use it within the structure of within-time space and matter. This remains a manipulation of the mind in its use, and therefore the mixing of two levels. This is neither right nor wrong. It is simply what often happens in situations where, for instance, magnetic healing and similar techniques are used, and where the boundaries are pushed out but still remain within the same limits.

Homer for instance spoke of the wine-coloured sea. He was able to see more than the spectrum of the seven colours as others could but, had he written about the purple that he saw, no-one would have understood this, so instead he used the expression 'wine-coloured' which people could relate to. This is an example of pushing out boundaries but remaining within certain limits.

For the last few years my curiosity has been centred in this place between in-time, space and matter (ie duality) and out-of-time space and matter. With the latter there is no duality but rather immediate action in the moment of thought and thereby pure transformation in the moment, not just change.

I am exploring the nature of what is between these two forms and what it is that in fact transforms in that moment, through the Metamorphic Technique and the astonishing enlightenment experienced through the words and conscious-ness of Gaston St Pierre. This is how the Metamorphic Asso-ciation describes the nature of their work:

> The Metamorphic Technique is a unique contribution to the holistic field where change, transformation and healing are sought. Instead of concentrating on symptoms or difficulties, the practitioner acts as a catalyst, providing the person who comes for a session with an inner environment free of direction, inter-ference and preconceived ideas. The power of life within the person guided by that person's innate intelligence can move his or her energy in the way that is necessary, directing the person to what feels right, such as a new diet or perhaps a change in work environment, an appropriate physical exercise or the right thera-peutic intervention.
>
> The earth will act as a catalyst for the seed and it is the energy within the seed that will put down roots and put up a shoot. These two elements will draw to the budding plant the necessary nourishment. There is need for contact between the earth and the seed. With the Metamorphic Technique, that contact is estab-lished through the practitioner touching lightly the spinal reflex points on the feet, hands and head.
>
> Because of its simplicity and the fact that a session is usually very pleasant and relaxing, many people are happy to use this technique every week as a tool for transformation and realization of their potential.

I understand that this transformational movement of energy takes place out of time, space and matter, and Gaston, in his exploration of the movement of these different energies, gives the following example.

We put food into our mouth which is an activity on one

level, in chewing it we change it to something different, but when we swallow it it no longer remains the food, but it has been transformed into the substance of the body. What then prevents our automatically transforming the quality of the energy we live? Our minds – which are useful to us at the level of time, space and matter but are indeed useless to us at the level of unity – fight and struggle to control our lives and thereby prevent transformation. So what are the factors needed for this process? Firstly there is the necessary quality for movement of life which is intelligence. Then there is our belief system, of 'the caterpillar state of being', that has to go completely to become a butterfly. This we find difficult to do: our minds attempt to control, and to keep the status quo by thinking and planning and maintaining the past. These fixing and controlling qualities are based on the past and future but do not include the present.

Our thinking is of the past, and our planning is in the future, and in our attention to yesterday and tomorrow we kill the creativity of today and of now. Our unconsciousness is only our consciousness, taken in at a subliminal level and held by the mind trapped in doubt. Intuition when it acts in us is like a laser striking directly from the heart, so that all the levels of us act simultaneously. Mostly our minds are engaged in patterns of memories, by which we unconsciously live our lives according to old beliefs. Beyond time is eternity, beyond space is infinity, and beyond form is the absolute. These are concepts for exploration, so what on earth are we doing then in so-called 'helping others'? In saying all this to attempt to help another is useless, yet somewhere within those that come to me there is a resonance to my work, or they would not come.

As the earth does not give to the plant but rather it is the plant that takes what it needs from its contact with the earth, so when clients make contact with me they take what they need for their own transformation. Even in the resonance alone something has happened: a change has taken place. I remember many years ago, when I would telephone Ingrid Lind for an astrological consultation, something would shift within the problem before I ever reached her and the appointment. This had nothing to do with our conversations, but rather with the contact of our voices. It was as if the problem cleared on that, and in a way the visit became not really necessary.

In just the same way, a client rang recently for an appointment saying she had undergone a complete breakdown which no one appeared to be able to help her through in spite of her being in a clinic, and she could not do it herself, her fear was too great. Now she had resorted to anti-depressants and was extremely unhappy; she had returned home, but was unable to leave the house in her fears. In fact, she was desperate, wondering how to hold on to life. We made an appointment for someone to bring her to see me; and even then she said that without driving herself it might be more than she could manage since she feared to move at all.

The snow then came so she could not keep the appointment. Her level of despair at being trapped rose as we spoke on the telephone and I heard myself reply as if from beyond my mind, 'If the snows come to trap you in perhaps you can go through this yourself. Could you do that if I am at the end of the telephone to be your support?'

'You must know as much about techniques as I do,' I told her, 'probably more. Have you given yourself permission to die?' I asked.

'Yes,' she replied, 'and I am not going to, but I do not know how to live.'

I asked her if she could risk remaining with the feeling of the terror and allowing the pain, when it came, and I assured her that I knew from my own experience that at any point there was always choice. Over the telephone I answered her questions and shared with her my own experiences and those that I had gone through with others reclaiming what was trapped in that life-death no-man's land. I encouraged her to honour in herself her astonishing courage even to attempt facing those desperate levels of herself, and the isolation and the panic that it is necessary to go through to come back to life in a new way. This is a transformation, not just a change; it does not require the mind's intervention, and one is never that person in energy again.

Somehow I was able to give her the permission she needed to give herself, to do what she needed to do: a journey that perhaps those in the clinic caring for her had not themselves been through and therefore were unable to offer their support to her on the level that she needed. Most of us fear death in our society, so to challenge near-death is not yet possible. Her intelligence knew all along what it needed to do but whereas before she had been surrounded by fear, which in turn had crystallized her fear in dis-ease, now she was ready to find a catalyst that could meet her on the level of near-death. This time her journey was wholly successful and within a month she was back into life, driving in her car to see me and although still feeling fragile she was excited to be alive. The hardest thing, she said, was her mind getting used to this new person that had no need to control and fix others' lives as had been her need for so many years, due to her own early years of deprivation. Her journey back to herself will take time. My own return took three years.

In our suffering from limitations we are all patients, but at the level at which transformation takes place – there is nothing we can do for another – it becomes enough that there is the contact of energy. In this case it was our voices on the telephone. Once again I am reminded of Ilana's voice telling us to remember that the less we do the more will happen. Did she know what she too was exploring?

The only component able then to transform me is my own life-force. The transformation is permanent and it happens with no effort as it is indeed merely the life in me living to fulfil its potential more fully as a human being.

I have written earlier of how I find the patterns and memories carried in the different areas of the body. As I work on a physical level my hands work as a catalyst to loosen the structures of the body which is of time and matter. The life-force of that person can then move as necessary and transform. Life always works towards fulfilment of its highest potential and, as in nature, people change for the better not worse.

DYNAMIC CHANGE AND TRANSFORMATION

It is difficult to look beyond the physical and accept the possibility of transformation through doing nothing! What happens that causes people with confirmed, crystallized conditions to break free, catalysed, as I have said, by the practitioner? I have stood by while watching the energy do a dance of its own in the client's body as the levels unblocked, let go, gyrating from top to toe – with no pain.

I have felt this myself in my own transformation. It would happen mostly at night, before dawn (could this be my birth I was re-enacting in those hours in which I struggled and was trapped?) My body would begin to dance, going into the strangest positions, producing sounds from my throat which, had they been heard, I am sure I would have been locked up for producing! Yet far from being random, there seemed to have been an intelligence at work.

There was always a beginning phase, a middle and an end, a resolution in feelings of peace, safety and lightness. Clients undergoing the same unlocking speak of tiredness, with a heaviness in the sense of more bodily awareness; but the biggest shift is in attitude to life which becomes much easier and more willing.

I recently worked with a man in his fifties, diagnosed as having severe arthritis in his feet and ankles, slowly manifesting in his arms, wrists and hands. He had succumbed to a wheelchair to transport himself, as each time his feet were on the floor for any length of time, his lower legs, ankles and feet would swell up. No doctor had a solution, and the physiotherapy he was undergoing was causing acute pain and apparently little benefit.

'Look at them,' he said to me when we met, pointing to his feet. 'They are like two slabs of marble.'

In childhood this man had had two operations to his feet (to the tendons in the heel and lower arch). He had lost an elder brother in the war and his mother had died two years previously. He had been very close to and fond of her, particularly so since his brother had died, and she had had an operation that had confined her to a wheelchair.

This man's crystallized condition began to shift and change almost at once. I worked with my hands almost exclusively on his back in the early stages and gave him homework in the form of chosen Feldenkrais movements to be done daily. This he did with the methodical commitment that he applied to his profession and his feet began to change. We worked on, allowing the head in its own time to let go of its crystallized beliefs. Also at this time he chose to marry for the first time. Now, a year or so later, although stiffness and pain manifest when he is over-stretched, particularly in the lower back, knees and ankles, he is once again playing golf and walking the Scottish hills.

As the mind builds its trust in the body again, the body seems able with little effort to re-establish movement and ease from disease. This example is of how dynamic change can take place within the structure of Space and Matter. The further stage is that of transformation: to have knowledge at the point of experience, that where there is nothing (beyond mind) there is also everything. This is the mystery of life that we have forgotten how to listen to, and which therefore the mind mostly cannot risk.

In allowing the life-force to move under my hands, I have also gradually become able to see the energy. It is as if I can see an X-ray photograph: the darker patches and the interconnections. In this way it is so easy to 'go to the edge' without fear of breaking a limb or dislocating a joint, but rather releasing – possibly in the same way as a chiropractor might – the memory and energy thus trapped.

I now see the importance of our time before conception and through it into the womb which becomes the blueprint for our lives and experience on earth. At conception there is a separation from the unity of the universe in our coming to experience matter and, in another sense, a unity with our mother. At birth there is the separation from our mother and our unity with her, and again at death there is separation from life on earth and from whatever stage we have arrived at on our journey of transformation in living heaven on earth. There are also the many small separations we go through, such as school, relationships, and even the end of the day which gives way to the night's gestation period before another day.

In remembering the time of our foundations that released into life what we are now, we can understand its different qualities. In knowing the areas of the body that hold the different patterns this becomes possible. Add to that the knowledge that the pineal gland is the focal point for our intelligence out of time, space and matter to come together with life in time, space and matter as an 'idea'. The pituitary gland's function then is a step down, bringing this idea to manifest as life in the body – in short as a human being.

All that happens prior to conception is out of time, space and matter. Out of awareness and power coming together there is a deep communication; but out of simply believing in something which we do not test to find out if it is true or false, the mind has an opportunity to trap us in 'do not know'. This is the place of the status quo, our conditioning. The Church can use such means as the 'fear of hell', the 'hope of heaven' and the 'guilt of sin' to keep its followers in ignorance of finding out through their own experience. This, in my view, is a perversion of the original teachings given to man.

Psychology is involved with the evolution of matter, as are many therapies; on the other hand, our physicists now tell us all is crystallized light. To be free it is necessary to bring these two aspects of matter, and our light energy, together. Our ideas and ideals can so easily take us away from life and the present, as can to quest and to help. Since the beginning and the end are the same thing, there is nowhere to go: there is only now.

In helping others we help our own point of view. Remaining at home in ourselves, as Gaston says, enables the client to take what he or she needs and to ask the questions they need the answers to, leaving anything else to fall into a category of abuse. By this I mean abusing the others' intelligence. It is in stillness that we hear our answers.

To 'be well' is then but a point of view, but not necessarily a fact, and it is best to live with facts. If the mind remains still the cells can transform from inside. Looking back on my journey to myself I see how I went to the lectures and workshops first to listen, later to have, and lastly, as I integrated what I had learnt, it became part of me in my work with others, and my living of life. Now it is simply a laser-like shift of energy at a very subtle level. It happens in my body when and where it needs to. I do not interfere, but I do watch and I do listen out of curiosity at the extraordinary intelligence that is there at work unlocking life.

These principal standpoints were taught by Krishnamurti and also by Montessori and now by Gaston St Pierre, Robert St John and David Bohm and others like them.

It is after all the very patterns that I have become aware of that have given me the tools that I use in my work. What at the time I feared to be abnormal was in fact perfectly normal within the sphere of awareness at which I was operating at that time; and my crises triggered further consciousness.

You could say that the eating of the apple by Eve with Adam – eating of the Fruit of Knowledge, in other words the experience of knowing – gave a step up in consciousness that was vital to man's evolution.

It is thanks to my pain that I now fully realize what many adults must avoid all their lives, and I also feel I now understand why so many fail to confront their truth, preferring instead to live lives of denial and pretence which are in themselves hugely self-destructive. What is worse, still fewer know they are doing it.

Through those early married years I feel I used my children, albeit wholly unconsciously, to fulfil my egoistic wishes. I firmly believed they should behave my way, or my duty as a mother would not be fulfilled. In my growing up with so little sense of self-worth I certainly, in my unconscious craving for it, trained my children to give it to me.

For most of us then, that sensitive true self remains repressed and hidden throughout our lives, unless illness, relationships or depression and curiosity (for so I called it until I recognized my need) drive us to search out and then confront this stranger within us, in order to survive what at times feels like a state bordering on insanity. What gets suppressed gets blown up in a crisis situation which is lacking in dignity, is untidy and, of course, is shunned by society who label us unbalanced or histrionic. I expect if you have read this far you will feel and recognize all of it.

There is great loneliness in knowing one must live one's own particular life. Yet if that deep loneliness transforms into love, one is able to live through the loneliness that pain causes without being destroyed. 'Joy is deeper yet than agony,' Nietzsche says. There is indeed a joy deeper than sorrow and it is our pain that drives us on through to experience it.

The deep loneliness within the soul cannot be taken away by intimacy with another human being. It is a longing for communion with Life. We look for others to take away this deep loneliness, and become angry and disappointed in them and in ourselves for not being able to bring this about. Only alone can we walk into our darkness and depth, searching in our unknowingness for another dimension. The more we live in the now, connected to the experience, the more every activity can be lived and felt as a celebration – each meal, each conversation, even the washing up – and all of the struggles become a celebration of joy and life. We have a choice to make each activity utterly mundane, or to make it an expression of our joyous soul; living in the moment instead of the future.

I believe we can use our attunement to light to tune ourselves to a frequency that can walk through walls, rebuild amputated limbs and be in two or three places at once. If there is no resistance, there can be no blowing of a fuse. In the period of change-over from my hands and mind, working within a technique, to my letting go and to being the observer of what my hands would risk and the extraordinary results, I became very conscious of the presence and instruction of a particular healer living in Australia, and of his encouragement and guidance. There was also one other who seemed to be pulling me into another state of consciousness with his presence in the same way. After some months these presences didn't come to me any more, as if I were being initiated to another level of work. My hands have worked independently of me ever since. I would encourage anyone to risk this shift. It feels as if I am at the doorway of the limitless.

I have begun to explore sound and its effects on our being, and this is another very different example of attuning. Disco music and the lights of red and yellow can make one feel thoroughly nauseous and disorientated if resisted, but if you allow yourself to become one with the sound and colour no harm is done, since there is a merging not a separation. Alternatively, Gregorian chant was consciously written to awaken higher levels of perception. The lamas of Tibet chant from their bellies, presumably in an attempt to stay with their bodies, living as they do in such rarefied conditions.

When I began my practice, I used various different

techniques as I worked with people to open up awareness, but today I do not find it necessary to work within a structure. By allowing my hands to travel where they will, I become a listening observer through my fingers. The focus is on the client's readiness to allow the transformation, not on what I can change for them. My workshops on going beyond techniques 'create a place where others can do the same'. Many dramatic disclosures have surfaced and many people have lived through their own near-deaths, releasing a whole new quality into their lives.

In near-dying, experienced over a number of times, the consciousness begins to perceive life the other side of dying, as I did. Attitudes change, and there is a feeling of being one with the process, of letting go without fear, of simultaneously feeling the death and the new life emerging through the process of dying. It was extremely intriguing to me that an expansion of consciousness at such a level could take place, with my knowing that at all times it was I who was in the director's seat.

In our disconnection of one facet of ourselves from another we have forgotten what we know, and we punish ourselves for having forgotten. Once we remember again what we have always known, we will not need to die in pain or have to leave the body to know what we already know. Accidents and disease are not natural causes of death. They are the result of living against basic cosmic law.

The more we experience ourselves as energy the more we can 'tune' ourselves to the changing level of radiation that is already now increasing. We need to have bodies like sports cars, not station-wagons. Radiation is only light. If we 'spring-clean' well, it is not difficult to run at a different and faster frequency and still have our feet on the earth. If we cannot 'spring-clean', de-coke the system to a finer attunement of energy flow, then dis-ease results, instead of life.

In my sessions, the client's 'story' is of little importance; what is important are the patterns forming the themes – the archetypal patterns, as Lynn Buess calls them: our misuse of power; our attachment to being victims of life's circumstances; separation from life; not wanting to be on Earth; the father representing our doing, the mother our being. There are a few themes but many variations.

Why not experience the freeing of elation and joy at being alive, a losing of the outlines of the body as we interconnect with all life? A feeling of great safeness on waves of light, colour and sound of such incredible delicacy, yet steel-like strength. A sense of foreverness, yet of being still with the body.

I now feel in myself a lightness and joy I have not before experienced. Gone are the legs that could not stand, the tight chest, the days and nights of turmoil. Instead there is a steady calm, and with it deep understanding, acceptance and tranquillity, peace and contentment within myself. I feel I have come home with a huge gratitude that I am myself, and that I know the many wonderful people I do, who have played their part in this journey through the drama of my dis-ease to now rejoice in its ease. Life is not so much the pursuit of happiness, as the discovery of joy.

We can alter the disease in our fluids and change the oceans. We can alter the disease in our breath and connection to life and so change the skies. We can alter the disease in our structure and change the land masses. We come of the same substance. The microcosm changes the macrocosm.

We can help evolution of all living substance by starting with ourselves. Move into our multi-dimensional capacities and alter what has got them out of balance. As within so without. We can look at what is around us in daily life to get a good map of the interior of ourselves and start with ourselves to function satisfactorily as global beings.

The reassurance to listen within to our own knowing and follow it; a helping hand to risk being on the edge and to following our own truth. Isn't that what we all need from each other?

My vibration, or energy, dictates how I will work. I watch how, as once again my way of working changes in accordance with my inner transformation.

EPILOGUE

Be a light unto yourself

Wherever there is beauty, truth and love, there is God. Joy
unfolds, whereas happiness we acquire.

Light ushers in a new medicine, one that I believe can dramat-
ically change our lives. It brings together intuition with rational science. There is nowhere that light cannot penetrate. We
speak of the eyes as the mirror of the soul. At best the human
body can no longer be seen as a piece of equipment with
replaceable parts, but must now be recognized as a living
photocell.

With the energy of light today, old emotional patterns of
trauma can be transformed quicker and easier because of its
ability to reach the mind, body and soul simultaneously. Is
this then what is now being explored: the medicine that can
speed mankind into an age of enlightenment?

When I read back through this book, I feel I read back
through decades of myself. I entered my journey to transform
my disease, how much more I have discovered! I feel as if I
have been given a 'transfusion of light'. I now know this transfusion never came from outside but was the continual unfolding of myself from within.

There is still the eternal question of who is this 'myself' I
have journeyed to. In ending one cycle another has already
begun but I know now that true understanding and knowledge
come from a world beyond that which we normally listen to or

see and that disease is but a holding place, a place to wake up to reality in.

My new home is a converted Chapel full of golden light!